# Business Babble

# Business Babble

## A Cynic's Dictionary of Corporate Jargon

### DAVID · OLIVE

Illustrated by Barry Blitt

**JOHN WILEY & SONS, INC.**

New York · Chichester · Brisbane · Toronto · Singapore

In recognition of the importance of preserving what has been
written, it is a policy of John Wiley & Sons, Inc., to have
books of enduring value published in the United States
printed on acid-free paper, and we exert our best efforts
to that end.

Copyright © 1990, 1991 David Olive
Illustrations © 1990, 1991 Barry Blitt

First published by Key Porter Books Limited, Toronto, CANADA
Published by John Wiley & Sons, Inc., edition published in 1991

**Library of Congress Cataloging-in-Publication Data**

Olive, David.
    Business babble: a cynic's dictionary of corporate jargon / by
David Olive.
      p.     cm.
    Includes index.
    ISBN 0-471-54789-1
    1. Business—Dictionaries.  2. English language—Jargon.
3. Business—Quotations, maxims, etc.  I. Title.
HF1001.045  1991
650′.03—dc20                              91-9209

Printed in the United States of America

10 9 8 7 6 5 4 3 2 1

For my mother and father

# Contents

# *Preface*

> *The citizen of today is the victim of new forms of word magic so universal and so subtle that he is unable ever to escape their influence.*
>
> – C.K. OGDEN,
> CAMBRIDGE UNIVERSITY LANGUAGE SCHOLAR

STRIPPED TO ITS ESSENTIALS – A FEW PLYWOOD boxes, a brass hoop, a silk hat and a rabbit – there is not much magic to the work of the magician, whose sole object is to keep your attention on the trick, and away from the means by which it is performed. The magic, we well know, is in the credulity of the observer.

Fixing our gaze on a thriving enterprise, we sometimes are too ready to believe in the magic of commerce as we contemplate the daring, fortitude and persistence that are doubtless required of anyone who succeeds in transforming an idea into an industrial organization. It seems like magic, and it is – at least to the extent that illusion figures prominently in most forms of business activity. And most of the tricks are performed with words.

It is the rare entrepreneur, insisting that he will soon recover from an irksome period of "negative cash flow," who is eager for prospective suppliers to gain a precise knowledge of his or her financial status; the rare takeover artist, citing a desire to "realize operating synergies," who is prepared to acknowledge a near total ignorance of the company being acquired; the rare personnel manager, taking refuge in the benign term "census reduction," who would risk throwing an entire firm into a panic over the likelihood of massive job losses; and the rare CEO who finds "pollution" as easy a concept to justify as that of "adverse environmental impacts."

The successful businessperson is a skilled obscurantist. The tools of this trade are derived from war ("white knights," "naked to your enemies" and "missing in action"), sports ("groin pulls" and "tennis-court justice"), street crime ("Saturday Night specials"), sex ("performance anxiety") and the animal kingdom ("pigs," "bear hugs," "cash cows" "vulture funds" and "elephant-man strategies"). Among the favored sources of some of the newest terms are the worlds of politics ("plausible deniability" and "constructive ambiguity"), popular television ("sixtysomething") and computer science ("compusavants," "quant jocks" and "digitheads"). But regardless of the source of inspiration, each term suits the same purpose: each is a code word designed to alert only those in the know to the true state of affairs. The "bottom line," as the saying goes, is that nothing in business is quite as it seems. Which requires you, if you are to survive, never mind thrive, to learn the code or suffer the consequence of it working against you.

As in politics, the successful businessperson finds that candor is not a reliable method in winning trust, overcoming resistance and attaining goals. The football coach can instruct his players to go out there and *Kill, kill, kill!* An expression of admirable clarity, to be sure, but ill-advised in business, which survives on the appearance of mutual benefit and noble purpose. Thus all business activity is guided by ambiguity of means and motive. While the world of commerce never lacks for emperors with no clothes, most of these individuals are, of necessity, handy with a glib expression.

Behind the veil of "dislocations," "restructurings," "off-balance-sheet financings," "reality checks" and "management by walking around," business is exposed as a work of the imagination, a land of self-invented alacrity and acumen. The distinguished historian Barbara Tuchman said that war is the unfolding of miscalculations. Once we have separated what businesspeople mean from what they say, business is revealed as the unfolding of mistakes, overconfidence and unrealistic expectations. Better make that "errors in judgment," "courage" and much "anticipointment."

I offer this book to those who have not dared inquire into the implications of a recently announced "challenging transition period." I offer it in order that you can become a master of the words that shape your fate. When you have finished the book, you will appreciate perhaps more than you already do that words, not money, are the currency of business.

# Acknowledgments

I wish to thank the staff of Key Porter Books for their assistance in making this book possible; and to acknowledge the generosity of Marq de Villiers and *Toronto Life* for granting me a leave of absence to complete the work. My greatest debt is to my editor, Charis Wahl, who long ago won me over to her belief that many of our problems go unsolved only for want of a little constructive anarchism.

*"The question is," said Alice, "whether you can make words mean so many different things." "The question is," said Humpty-Dumpty, "which is to be master – that's all."*

– LEWIS CARROLL,
*THROUGH THE LOOKING-GLASS*

**abasement** *n.* The remedy of first resort in confronting a higher authority. On these occasions, it is best not to confuse the goals of justice and continued employment.

**ability** *n.* The tolerance shown by an employee for coping with superiors whose cognitive endowment would embarrass a tree stump.

**abnormal** *adj.* Business behavior that usually can be arrested if detected in its early stages. It includes a lack of interest in succeeding to the presidency; a weakness for family life; a detectable sympathy with trade unionism and the Democratic Party; and a tendency to use plain English when what's called for is the phrase "marginal capacity utilization."

**accommodate** *v*. 1. To give in to someone else's idea because that someone else could kick your can down the corporate ladder if you don't. Common usage: "The boss hates products with a high ticket price, so I'm launching this one with a low price. Of course, we'll lose a bundle on it at first. But once we get a decent market share, we can hike the price." 2. To win approval for a project by surrendering its merits, thus dooming the project to failure. Common usage: "Hear what happened to Bill with Project X? He gave in on everything – price, packaging and formulation. He's even changing the color to puce. He'll do really well with it – but not outside of Idaho."

**accommodation invoicing** *n*. Billing the company for your son's car, your mother's trip to the spa at Baden-Baden and the heliport behind your garage.

*A tremendous amount of business is discussed at activities like this. [It] isn't all just discussing how pretty the bride looks.* – Stanford C. Stoddard, former chairman of Michigan National Corp., explaining to a judge in 1986 why the company paid for the orchestra at his daughter's wedding reception

**accounting, creative** *n.* A free-style event noted for its lively and imaginative interpretations of reality. The successful creative accountant is able to depict liabilities as assets, losses as profits and feckless clients as pillars of probity.

*Two and two is four and five'll get you ten — if you know how to work it.* — Mae West

**accounts payable** *n.* Theirs.

**accounts receivable** *n.* Ours.

**acquisition** *n.* A new arrival. This is not the occasion, unlike the happy addition of a baby brother or sister, to ooh and ahh over the new family member. On a personal level, this is an occasion to wonder (a) about the shortcomings of your firm that drove it to adoption as a means of overcoming them, and the possibility that your own department figures into those shortcomings; and (b) whether you and your colleagues will get to run the acquisition, or instead be placed under the supervision of *its* team of star managers (which has come in for heavy praise, of course, by way of justifying the acquisition). In the larger corporate picture, this is a time for sober reflection on the inflated expectations that attend dealmaking. A time to note, for instance, that "acquisition" is a word with twice as many syllables as "purchase" – an early hint of complications to follow. By the same logic, "divestiture" has four times the syllables of "sale."

**acronym** *n.* 1. The tangible acknowledgment by a firm, often in the aftermath of an acquisition binge, that it no longer is entirely certain what line of business it is in. 2. The tangible acknowledgment of the lines of business a firm would *like* to be in – or the stock market would like it to be in. Hence the transformation of Acme Widgets Corp. to AWC Technologies Corp. in the 1970s; to AWC Resources Corp. in the 1980s; and AWC Environmental Sciences Corp. in the 1990s. The device finds its most favorable application in those instances where the temptation to transform the firm to fit its new name is successfully resisted. (See **acquisition**)

**activist shareholder** *n.* A raider.

*Activist shareholders come forth to do battle for control of misman-*

*aged corporations and to put the assets of these corporations to better uses.* – T. Boone Pickens, raider of Gulf Oil, Phillips Petroleum, Unocal Corp. and other firms

*Were they really Robin Hood and his Merry Men, as they claimed? Or were they Genghis Khan and the Mongol hordes? ... I don't see the raiders creating jobs. I don't see them boosting productivity. And worst of all, I don't see them doing a single thing to help America compete in the world.* – Lee Iacocca

**administrivia** *n.* The necessary precondition to executive action.

*I can't stand this proliferation of paperwork. It's useless to fight the forms. You've got to kill the people producing them.* – Vladimir Kabaidze, general director of the Ivanovo Machine Building Works near Moscow, at a Communist Party conference in 1988

**adverse market conditions** *n.* A total absence of the favorable conditions that until now concealed most of our mistakes.

**advertising** *n.* Words and pictures, often set to music, designed to correct the mistaken impression among consumers that their lives possess meaning in the absence of a receipt for a particular product in their sock drawer.

*Advertising may be described as the science of arresting the human intelligence long enough to get money from it.* – Stephen Leacock

*Half the money I spend on advertising is wasted, and the trouble is, I don't know which half.* – John Wanamaker, American dry-goods retailer

*The consumer is not a moron. She's your wife.* – David Ogilvy, cofounder of ad agency Ogilvy & Mather

**advertising slogan** *n.* A memorable expression whose effectiveness can be gauged according to how little substance it conveys.

*Kronenberg – a beer that doesn't taste as if it had a dead rat in it.* – ad slogan created for the French brewer in 1985 by British comedian John Cleese

**agenda** *n.* A control mechanism for ruling inappropriate ideas out of order.

**aggressive** *adj.* 1. Investing posture favored by brokers, in which the client commits his net worth to the market and his better judgment to the four winds. 2. In abnormal psychology, a character trait associated with unattractive or self-destructive behavior; in business, a widely celebrated prerequisite to career success. 3. Label for a woman who is doing her job well, and so has become the focus of resentment from both male and female peers. It is this person who inspires the adage: If you want a job done, get a man; if you want it done right away, get a woman.

**ally** *n.* A colleague who, in large meetings, helpfully greets your idea with an apparently spontaneous outburst of enthusiasm, and marvels at your heroic advancement of the company's interests in packed elevators. There is a caveat: As long as his reputation is sound, he can cheerlead; once he has a cloud over his head, his only link with you is that gift subscription to *Field & Stream*.

**ambition** *n.* The spur to folly.

**amortization** *n.* The reduction and retirement of a dream by way of payments to the bankers who hold it hostage. (See **Campeau factor**)

**annual meeting** *n.* A sacred rite of corporate democracy in which the CEO, sweating audibly, invites the slings and arrows that might naturally arise from his recent outrageous misfortunes. His self-sacrifice is averted by an interminable, upbeat audio-visual presentation prior to the session, which numbs participants into passivity; and the announcement that exotic refreshments are available in an adjoining room, irresistible to all but the most determined and self-righteous questioners.

*A year is that period required to make one or two catastrophic mistakes, to entrench some habits, and above all to leave much awaiting conclusion.* – Richard Todd, in the *New England Monthly*

**annual report** *n.* An overdesigned catalogue of managerial triumphs, not wholly undermined by a companion index of statistics, whose obscure depiction of the firm's decayed financial state is yet another triumph of its kind.

**anticipointment** *n.* High expectations among consumers prior to the appearance of a new product punctured by equally severe disappointment upon its arrival. The term, which originated in the entertainment business in the late 1980s, appears to have been inspired by early viewer response to "The Pat Sajak Show."

**anti-suit** *n.* An individual heralded for his disarming personality and "creative streak," whose capacity for mischief is obscured by his or her casual dress and an apparent indifference to playing by the book. (See **suit**)

**appreciation** *n.* Vindication.

**asset, core** *n.* A corporate asset not yet considered dispensable. Also called "strategic asset."

**asset disposition program** *n.* A fire sale. There are two types of fire sale at the corporation pressed for cash: the kind that begins with an official announcement that "This is not a fire sale"; and an "asset disposition program."

**asset, non-core** *n.* An asset described as no longer essential to the company's "basic" or "core" business, at the same moment its neck is being fitted for a price tag. Ninety-eight percent of the time, the asset being shipped to the auction block is no longer "strategic" because it is a chronic underperformer – but, then, that's no way to talk up something you're trying to sell. (See **dog**)

**asset shuffle** *n.* A widespread practice resembling the negotiating of draft choices in professional sport, in which companies propose giving up certain divisions and subsidiaries in exchange for those of other companies in a bid to enhance the performance of the transformed firm. In this way, management is becoming ever less the art of running a business than of adroitly trading its component parts.

**asset stripping** *n.* An exercise in financial surgery, commonly performed on a takeover target by its acquisitor, which consists of removing and selling various parts of the company in order to recover the cost of its acquisition. The exercise is complete when the assets remaining are debt, debt payments and demoralized employees.

**assignment, special** *n.* The Siberian exile of an executive in order to remove him from the scene of his mistakes, inertia or politically incorrect behavior.

**assistant, administrative** *n.* The only person who knows the CEO's exact mood and whereabouts at all times. Also, the individual who reads your blistering confidential memos to the CEO; and the Cerberus who decides whether your cause is sufficiently pressing to justify penciling you in for an audience with Himself.

**attrition** *n.* A compassionate alternative to layoffs, whereby you get to keep your job *and* it's more fulfilling – as now you work half again as hard as you did before the others quit.

**audit lapse** *n.* A condition that arises when management, preoccupied with building for the future, skillfully neglects to ensure that the books reflect fiscal misfortune and malfeasance past and present.

*The reaction of weak managements to weak operations is often weak accounting. The Yanomano Indians employ only three numbers: one, two and more than two. Maybe their time will come.* – Warren Buffett, billionaire investor

**auditor's report** *n.* A comforting paragraph or two from the outside auditor to say that the financial statements prepared by its client – whom it would very much like to keep as a client – appear to conform with "generally accepted accounting principles" (GAAP). It remains for the shareholders, regulators and police to determine the potential entertainment value of these statements in a criminal proceeding.

**austerity, positive** *n.* A mild cost-cutting drive that claims a few jobs elsewhere in the company, in contrast to a rationalization, which claims yours.

**back office** *n.* The place where the order that your broker urged you to make today without a moment to lose takes four months to process.

**bag of snakes** *n.* An acquisition which, had it only been less than it was talked up, you could have lived with, but instead is full of venomous surprises.

**bankruptcy** *n.* An occasion for surrendering pride to a judge; chiefly notable for the many enterprises that somehow avoid it, and the many entrepreneurs who survive it with their fortunes enhanced.

*Our revels now are ended.* – William Shakespeare

**bankster** *n.* A term whose revival is long overdue, coined by *Time* in the 1930s for the agents whose scheming precipitated a string of bank collapses at the dawn of the Depression.

**bargain** *n.* A transaction in which both parties are satisfied that their interests have been served, except that one became richer.

*When the white man came, we had the land and they had the bibles. Now they have the land and we have the bibles.* – Chief Dan George

**bargain purchase folly** *n.* Disregard for the truism that you get what you pay for.

*The original "bargain" price probably will not turn out to be such a steal after all. In [acquiring] a difficult business, no sooner is one problem solved than another surfaces – never is there just one cockroach in the kitchen.* – Warren Buffett

**bean counter** *n.* An initiative thwarter who wields tyrannical power over the paper-clip budget, but who is not permitted into the executive suite, where the billion-dollar bungles are conceived.

**bear hug** *n.* A welcome embrace by one company coming to the rescue of another fending off a hostile takeover; this display of affection soon tightens into a death grip as the putative rescuer makes a meal of the rescuee.

**bed down** *v.* In the aftermath of a takeover, the determination of who gets the covers and who sleeps on the side closest to the bathroom.

*New York securities dealer Shearson Lehman Bros. developed a handbook for digesting rival brokerage E.F. Hutton & Co. that broke down the merger into some 1,200 steps, including a directive to "look for toaster for Tuesday morning staff meeting." –* news report, *The Globe and Mail*

**before? Didn't we try this once** *phrase.* Translation: No.

**bells and whistles** *n.* Noisy peripherals that distract the purchaser's attention from the price.

**belly-up** *adj.* Term for a capsized enterprise, whose scarred underside is no longer visible only to creditors.

**benefactor** *n.* A financier who favors selected unthreatening charities with a modest portion of the largess extended to his own company by the public. The benefactor acquires the comforting knowledge that future generations may associate his name with pursuits loftier than those by which he made his living.

*Base wealth preferring to eternal praise.* – Homer

*Cain took care not to commit another murder, unlike our railway shareholders (I am one) who kill and maim shunters by hundreds to save the cost of automatic couplings, and make atonement by annual subscriptions to deserving causes.* – George Bernard Shaw

**beneficial owner** *n.* The person on whose behalf an agent representing a numbered firm incorporated in Montevideo controls an enterprise which operates as a division of a Swiss-based holding company.

**bile factor** *n.* A layoff policy's legacy of accumulated ill will.

*Over the years the relentless pressure of cost cutting had created within Heinz a mounting feeling of bile. The notion that when people on high exhort you to cut costs they're talking about cutting your costs, not theirs, bred distaste. There was an ever-increasing feeling of hostility among the employees. Fewer people do more work. Layoffs create a degree of insecurity because workers wonder if 50 people were cut last year and 100 this year, how many will go next year?* – Anthony O'Reilly, CEO of H.J. Heinz

**black dream** *n.* 1. The realization of your worst enemy's most grotesque scheme, revealed to you during your slumbers in graphic, Hitchcockesque detail. 2. The realization of your own most grotesque scheme, revealed to your sworn enemies in their slumbers, the character representing you being brilliantly acted by Alan Bates.

**blame, No one is suggesting you're to** *phrase.* Translation: You are to blame. You will make it up to me. (See **fault**)

**blame-time** *n.* The witch-hunting hour.

*There is no more feared hour in the corporate world than blame-time … To blame someone is to injure him verbally in public; in large organizations where one's image is crucial to one's "credibility" and therefore one's influence, this poses the most serious sort of threat … As a general rule, when blame is allocated, it is those who are or become politically vulnerable or expendable who become "patsies," who get "set up" or "hung out to dry" and become blamable.* – Robert Jackall, *Moral Mazes*

**bleeding edge** *n.* The dividing line between a management layer that no longer exists and the one above it, which anxiously awaits news of another attempt to "realize operating efficiencies."

**blue chip** *n.* Shares in a company that has not yet been subjected to a leveraged buyout. (See **buffalo chip** and **red chip**)

**blue sky** *v.* To conceptualize freely with no effort to make ideas conform to economic and other realities.

**board of directors** *n.* A curious body whose members are selected on the recommendation of the CEO, over whom they have supervisory powers. Members unfailingly err on the safe side of this contradiction, modeling their behavior on politburos and presidential cabinets – where rebelling against the CEO is marginally less practical.

*Went to the yearly court of the Edinburgh Assurance Co., to which I am one of those graceful and useless appendages called "Directors Extraordinary."* – diary notation in 1825 of Sir Walter Scott, who was driven to near penury when held responsible for the debts of a bankrupt firm of which he was a director. Today, things are different.

*There is one thing all boards have in common ... they do not function.* – Peter Drucker

*Directors run virtually no personal risk for any amount of complacency, cronyism, or outright neglect of their duties. While the law holds [directors] responsible as fiduciaries to the stockholders, the courts have interpreted that responsibility very leniently. A director would rarely be found liable unless cupidity, a clear conflict of interest, or gross negligence (a vague concept) could be proved. Even then, he is usually further protected by his company's indemnification and insurance policies, which in effect guarantee that any damages assessed against him will be paid by the company.* – Harold Geneen, former CEO of ITT Corp., in his book, *Managing*

**boesky** *v.* To hoodwink fellow investors, turn state's evidence, do a little time and emerge from prison as an investment counsellor. (See **tennis-court justice**)

**boesky-constrictor** *n.* A state prosecutor whose job is to bring insider traders to justice and himself to the voters' attention.

**boiler room** *n.* 1. An office, usually located in the Caribbean or another jurisdiction safe from U.S. extradition treaties, from which unscrupulous brokers contact hapless investors in North America or Europe by telephone in an effort to peddle worthless securities to them. 2. The CEO's office, where medium-rare subordinates are separated from the extra well-done.

**bond** *n.* 1. A kinship or other special tie between individuals. 2. A financial commitment between a company and an investor of a more exacting nature than the above relationship, except in the event of bankruptcy.

*Gentlemen prefer bonds.* – Andrew Mellon

**boom** *n.* A momentary lapse in the collective sanity of a market, during which the promise of something for nothing prevails over the law that insists what goes up must come down.

*Men, it has been well said, think in herds; it will be seen that they go mad in herds, while they only recover their senses slowly, and one by one.* – Charles Mackay, *Extraordinary Popular Delusions and the Madness of Crowds*

*I have always thought that if in 1929 we had all continuously repeated "two and two still make four," much of the evil might have been averted.* – Bernard Baruch

**borrowing power** *n.* Credulity of bankers.

**bottom line** *n.* The figure representing hope minus reality.

**boycott** *n.* An organized effort by consumers to express displeasure with a firm by not purchasing its products. The term originates with Charles Boycott, a nineteenth-century Irish land agent who suffered a tenant revolt when he refused to reduce rents. Boycotts, while an interesting phenomenon, tend to be of limited effect. The current boycott of the American automobile industry in favor of cars made in other countries, for instance, has not stopped Detroit from turning out products that no one wants.

**broad-gauged** *adj.* Responsive to new and unorthodox ideas. Common usage: "I told Jim we were thinking of converting his widget-stamping line over to edible inner fashions, and he thought it was worth trying. Turns out he's pretty broad-gauged."

**budgeting, strategic** *n.* A means of gaining approval for audacious proposals, by which a modest surplus is projected in full knowledge that a staggering deficit is more likely.

**buffalo chip** *n.* A blue-chip company that has been subjected to a leveraged buyout. During the settlement of the American West, destitute pioneers gathered buffalo chips for use as fuel. The recent proliferation of share certificates in former blue chips has created a similar, environmentally sound source of heat but little light.

**bum** *n.* Alternative to hero. In business, you learn there is no "yesterday's hero." You are either a hero or a bum.

*The idol of to-day pushes the hero of yesterday out of our recollection; and will, in turn, be supplanted by his successor of to-morrow.* – Washington Irving

**burning-bush syndrome** *phrase.* Management style of the CEO in direct communication with a higher source of wisdom only he can tap, and whose edicts are backed up by punishment that would make an eye for an eye seem like time off for good behavior.

**business** *n.* Purposeful activity, derived from "busyness" – that is, full of sound and fury, signifying profit or loss.

*Business? It's quite simple. It's other people's money.* – Alexandre Dumas the Younger

*The growth of a large business is merely a survival of the fittest. The American beauty rose can be produced in the splendor and fragrance which bring cheer to its holder only by sacrificing the early buds*

*which grow up around it. This is not an evil tendency in business. It is merely the working out of a law of nature and a law of man.*
– John D. Rockefeller Jr.

**busymeet** *n.* A pow-wow that fills the empty hours that might otherwise be occupied with getting some work done.

**buyback** *n.* The purchase by a company of its own shares, often at the gentle encouragement of a major shareholder threatening to accumulate enough shares to oust management and scatter the firm's assets. (See **leveraged buyout**)

**buzz** *n.* Institutionalized gossip calculated to ignite "spontaneous" word-of-mouth interest about a new product prior to its appearance.

**Campeau factor** *n.* The suspected cause of a precipitous decline in a company's stock-market value, triggered by fear among investors that the firm, by taking on massive amounts of debt, has put ego before prosperity.

*People are thinking, here's another Canadian entrepreneur who's ... going to get blown out. That's the Canadian way.* – Ted Rogers, Canadian cable-TV magnate, citing what he called "the Campeau factor" for a decline in the value of his own company's shares in late 1989

*Think of Honda making cars in Ohio. People who would normally join the UAW are back at work. But the design is all done by Japanese, the engineering is all in Japan. We end up having the Canadian complaint. About half of Canadian manufacturing is foreign-owned, so Canadians don't get to compete for the top jobs. The best they can aspire to is CEO of a division.* – Lester Thurow, dean of the Sloan School of Business at the Massachusetts Institute of Technology, in *Fortune*

**candophobia** *n.* Fear of candor.

*Never believe anything until it has been officially denied.* – Otto von Bismarck

*Partially offsetting these increases was a drop in sales and profits associated with the space shuttle program.* – Charles Locke, chairman of Morton Thiokol, builder of space shuttle booster rockets, referring to the Challenger disaster in an upbeat third-quarter report

**candor** *n.* A bid for sympathy often mistaken for contrition.

*The decision went beyond dumb and reached all the way out to stupid.* – Lee Iacocca in 1987, on his company having sold as new cars that had been damaged during testing

*The entire Company reorganized its work force following the loss of 400 employees due to early retirement and attrition. Oil, gas, and*

*natural gas liquids prices collapsed across the board ... Northeastern Oklahoma flooded in October, creating havoc for the Company's service area. Two months later in the dead of winter, a transmission pipeline ruptured in Muskogee, Oklahoma, causing the biggest gas outage in the Company's history ... Even an unusually high number of meter readers were getting attacked by dogs ... As for 1987, we're glad it's over.* – excerpt from 1987 annual report of Oneok Inc., a Tulsa-based pipeline company

*We think Next will be the best possible company if every single person working here understands the whole basic master plan and can use that as a yardstick to make decisions ... The most visible sign of the open corporation at Next is our policy of allowing everybody to know what salary everybody else is making. There's a list in the finance department, and anyone can go look at it.* – Steve Jobs, founder of Apple Computer and Next Inc.

**cannibalize** *v.* An unfortunate mishap that occurs when your new product steals market share from your other products, instead of the competition's.

**cannon, loose** *n.* 1. An unpredictable middle manager best avoided lest you be swept into his folly. 2. An erratic tycoon such as Robert Campeau whose perpetual romance with folly is held in high respect by the investment bankers who make their living from it.

**capacity, excess** *n.* A dearth of sagacity.

*Excess capacity isn't some cataclysmic event that falls equally on all companies. They don't all wake up one morning and decide to close a factory. It is a cataclysmic event that falls on the company with the least competitive product.* – Maryann Keller, U.S. auto industry analyst

**capital** *n.* Money dressed for success. "Money" is loaded with unseemly connotations and fails to convey a sense of noble mission. Thus, a worthy corporate venture deserves an adequate "capital expenditure program" to ensure its success. By contrast, there's no point "sinking more money" into a lost cause, or fixing something that's beyond repair by "throwing more money at it." (See **earnings**)

**capitalism** *n.* A system in which responsibility for redistributing wealth is held to be more suitably entrusted to the supermarket than the legislature.

*The paradox of capitalism is that it is most successful when most dynamic; and when most dynamic, it is most destructive. It is, in Joseph Schumpeter's famous phrase, a system of "creative destruction." In its purest form, it is Darwinism, and meant to be so.* – editorial, *The Washington Post*

**cash cow** *n*. A division or subsidiary that makes such satisfying profits the parent company sees no need to reinvest those profits to keep the operation up to date; a safe dumping ground for executive deadwood. A cash cow "starved" is gradually transformed into a dog.

**cash flow** *n*. Money coming in, to the surprise of some and the relief of all.

**cash-flow deficiency** *n*. More money going out than coming in; man the lifeboats. Also called "negative cash flow."

**cassandra, corporate** *n*. A professional prophet of doom who cashes in on his or her forecasts of economic collapse with "crisis-investing" books offering tips on how to build a bomb shelter for your investments. If their track record is any guide, the more apocalyptic the vision, the brighter the immediate prospects for investment.

*Nuclear war would really set back cable-TV.* – Ted Turner, broadcasting magnate

**cat–eat–cat** *adj.* A term used to describe the efforts of Mrs. Alfred Everett-Hampton to ensure that more "names" turn out for her $500-a-plate charity ball than for the fundraiser being held across town the same evening by Mrs. Jonathan Welk-Strickland III.

*Like a manager eyeing the executive suite, she must work her way to the top through years of service in the trenches of volunteering— licking envelopes here, arranging flowers there ... Says* Globe and Mail *social columnist Rosemary Sexton, "You have to come up with great ideas and marshal the troops. Then when you rise above the crowd, you have to withstand the nail-clawing and backbiting ... – Report on Business Magazine*

**cause-related marketing** *n.* A philanthropic method by which firms are spared the inconvenience of parting with their own funds when rushing to the assistance of worthy causes. The device was pioneered in the late nineteenth century by New York *World* publisher Joseph Pulitzer, who reaped enormous gains in circulation from a brilliant campaign in which he exhorted the citizenry to donate pennies toward the construction of a ten-story base for the Statue of Liberty. The phenomenon was revived (and given its current name) by American Express Co. in 1983, when it conceived the idea of donating one cent from each purchase made with an AmEx card to refurbish that same statue.

**cautiously, I like your idea, but we must proceed** *phrase*. Translation: You must be joking. Come back in five years.

**cc:** *v*. Translation: 1. Whatever you may think of this idea, I've spared you the inconvenience of stealing credit for it. 2. I haven't gone over your head, but from now on the fact that you're a jerk is no longer our little secret.

**census reduction** *n*. Mass layoffs, an effort to fire as many people as possible.

**chairman** *n*. A former CEO who has been put out of the company's misery by elevating him to a rarified position of no responsibility. The ultimate special assignment.

**chairman, vice-** *n*. A post into which someone once thought to be CEO material has been shunted prior to retirement. Sometimes called deputy chairman.

**chief environment officer** *n.* A senior executive who has been put in charge of worrying about the firm's impact on the environment, in order that his colleagues might be spared this inconvenience. This is not the outdoor job it appears to be: the environment officer spends most of his or her time communing not with nature but with legislative subcommittees and delegations of environmental activists.

**chief executive officer (CEO)** *n.* God. The supreme decision-maker in the company, accountable only to the board of directors, to which he controls the flow of misinformation about the firm's affairs. The CEO is always right. His jokes are always funny. The people around him know what they're going to say even before he says it.

*An institution is the lengthened shadow of one man.* – Ralph Waldo Emerson

**chief executive, office of the** *n.* A tenuous arrangement in which ultimate power is shared, usually among three persons: the chairman, the president and the chief operating officer. Triumvirates are inherently unstable; in the wake of Julius Caesar's death, the triumvirs Mark Antony, Octavius and Lepidus were compelled to dispatch themselves to the far ends of the Roman Empire to keep from killing one another, and even this only postponed the inevitable bloodshed. Modern management by trio most often arises when a company's board of directors cannot decide who should run the firm, and is content to let the contenders duke it out for the privilege.

**chief financial officer (CFO)** *n*. The cash king, charged with bringing the CEO's rich schemes into rough alignment with the company's ability to fund them. Should this mission fail, the schemes may be scrapped; the CFO will be scrapped.

**chief information officer (CIO)** *n*. A data king. While nominally in charge of one of the two company assets (the other is money), the CIO is too much of a computer nerd to be taken seriously as a future CEO.

**chief operating officer (COO)** *n*. The CEO's chief lieutenant. If leading members of the board of directors share his view that he is the CEO's heir apparent, his behavior is worth monitoring to gauge what the next dictatorship will bring.

**Chinese wall** *n*. A staged undertaking by a brokerage's salespeople that they will not tout stocks that the underwriting department is desperate to unload. Nor will they sell the Eiffel Tower to a client unless he really, really wants to buy it.

*Chinese walls didn't keep the Mongols out of China, and they haven't kept the miscreants on Wall Street out of the honey pot either.* – John Dingell (D-Mich.), chairman of the House commerce committee

**churning** *n.* A practice in which the client of a brokerage is surprised to discover that in the past year he has owned a piece of 560 different companies.

**circumspection** *n.* A quality that recommends itself to the successful executive.

*I have noticed that nothing I never said ever did me any harm.* – Calvin Coolidge

**class action** *n.* The lynch mob.

**coattail provision** *n.* A corporate bylaw requiring that the small shareholders be bought out at the same time as the firm's majority owner, so that they, too, might benefit from an acquirer's inflated assessment of the company's value.

**cold call** *n.* The act of attempting to sell something to a person who hasn't heard of you, your company or your product.

*For a salesman, there is no rock bottom to the life ... He's a man way out there in the blue, riding on a smile and a shoeshine. And when they start not smiling back – that's an earthquake.* – Arthur Miller

**collectible** *n.* A baseball card, comic book or antique Coca-Cola bottle deemed to be a tangible store of wealth in times of rampant inflation. Collectible booms predict economic busts. When people put more faith in rusted railroad rails than shares of IBM, it's time to dust off your resume.

**comfort letter** *n.* An accountant's opinion that a financial statement appears to be on the up-and-up; designed to calm the nerves of a skeptical party to a proposed deal.

**comfort zone** *n.* The latitude of luxury in which an executive is permitted to operate, taking in first-class airline travel, company cars, baseball tickets and as many overpriced meals as he can eat. In time of inverted buoyancy, the comfort zone contracts: the cars are sold, mandatory annual checkups replace memberships at the posh fitness salon, and pup tents are issued for use on business trips.

**commodity** *n.* An investment vehicle whose awesome destructive qualities are less readily apparent in the field or the stable than on the floor of the Chicago Mercantile Exchange.

**compensation** *n*. An exact science rewarding each according to his clarity of goals, unshakable resolve and soundness of means. Thus did the chief executive of sneaker outfit Reebok International pull down $15.4 million in 1989, and the chief executive of the United States, $200,000.

**competition** *n*. A rivalry between two or more companies to attain such dominance of the market that competition ceases to exist.

*As the century's gaudy history of cartels and price agreements and tariffs demonstrates, businesspeople have exercised considerable ingenuity in avoiding unrestricted competition. Little wonder. Competition makes life turbulent and uncertain; competition almost always eats into profits. Worse, you can lose at competition.* – Charles C. Mann, *Atlantic Monthly*

**compromise** *n*. The art of surrendering with the greatest reluctance to those aspects of the other person's point of view that you find agreeable. Mort Sahl recalls that Henry Kissinger once allowed to the acceptability, on hearing the cries of a man drowning twenty feet away, of throwing him a fifteen-foot rope. "The President," Kissinger would say, "has met you more than halfway."

**compusavant** *n.* A person of prodigious mathematical ability, whose talents and personality invite comparison to a pocket calculator. Fortunately, the compusavant usually poses no threat in the truly important areas: power wardrobe, racquet sports and making rude suggestions to members of the opposite sex. (See **digithead**)

**concept company** *n.* An idea listed on a minor stock exchange.

**confidant** *n.* An individual upon whom the CEO relies for sage advice and for letting him cheat on his golf score.

**conglomerate** *n.* Capitalism's answer to the circus, operating on the premise that if the trapeze artist fails to impress the audience, the juggler will. In practice, at least some of the acts fail to please most of the time, and even the reliable crowd-pleasers slip eventually for lack of the ringmaster's wholehearted attention.

*If you have a harem of 40 women, you never get to know any of them very well.* – Warren Buffett

**consensus** *n.* The precaution of ensuring that you are not alone in holding to the strength of a conviction.

*In the multitude of counsellors, there is safety.* – Proverbs 11:14

**consent degree** *n*. A common form of plea bargaining in which a company pays a small fine to avoid big trouble. The street-level equivalent is a bank robber who allows that he may or may not be guilty, submits to a modest fine, and agrees to give no further thought to bank robbery as a career choice.

**constructive ambiguity** *n*. A phrase that does not alert you to the apocalypse that might not happen, point to a solution that may not work, or impart with clarity an explanation that may not be accurate.

*If the price of conventional [oil] is X, you have a price of X plus Y for the nonconventional oil, and the international price – you know what that is – but we have indicated we will continue to subsidize the prices ... so that what you would end up with would be a mix of these prices.* – Energy Minister Marc Lalonde, explaining Canadian oil policy to the House of Commons

**consultant** *n*. A mercenary who gracefully accepts your money to find merit in your sound proposal.

*When we ask for advice, we are usually looking for an accomplice.* – Marquis de Lagrange

*A consultant is someone who borrows your watch to tell you the time; a consultant is someone who knows a hundred ways to make love but doesn't know any girls.* – David Owen

**consumer product, post-** *n.* Recycled waste which only proves once again that what goes around comes around, usually overpriced and bearing a green label.

**contract** *n.* A handshake that will stand up in court.

*You can't have an adversary, me-first mentality and get a just-in-time production program or an R&D joint venture to work. We must learn to evolve from a contractually oriented business culture where if it's not in the contract, we do whatever the hell we want ... A Japanese contract is so vague it's unenforceable in U.S. courts. It says, well, the two of us will get together, and we think we're going to do this product, but if that doesn't work for us, then we'll have to change the terms of the agreement, because why would we want to go ahead with it and do it if it was killing us?* – Leonard Greenhalgh, instructor in negotiating at Dartmouth's Amos Tuck School of Business Administration, in *Fortune*

**contract out** *v.* 1. To farm out activities once done within the firm, as a way of making workers think again about their unrealistic wage demands. 2. The liberal use of lawyers, consultants and investment bankers to do a corporation's thinking.

**contrarian** *n.* An individual who correctly adduces that the pickings are better in the field that no one is standing in.

*The cleverly expressed opposite of any generally accepted idea is worth a fortune to somebody.* – F. Scott Fitzgerald

**controversy** *n.* A disturbance in which the interests of the press are at odds with a corporation's natural instinct to sit in sole judgment of its unimpeachable behavior.

**corporate culture** *n.* The defining ethic of a company, expressed in the speech, dress and behavior deemed proper at the firm, which are carefully designed to ward off the incursion of dangerous new ideas.

*The [Detroit] car men incessantly discuss how their relatives or close associates like or dislike the new models they are driving. Neither the cost nor the maintenance of these cars reflect the reality of owning and operating an automobile in America. Many of the cars have been obtained through special management buy/lease programs, or they belong to vast, painstakingly maintained corporate pools. The corporations discourage young executives from driving the cars of their competitors – or even renting them on business trips. It is as if the president of the United States were to judge commercial air travel based on his flights aboard Air Force One.* – Brock Yates, *The Decline and Fall of the American Automobile Industry*

**corporate social responsibility (CSR)** *n.* A management theory that suggests if business apologizes from time to time for its alleged moral shortcomings, it, and not government, will determine the pace at which these may be abandoned for new ones.

*Grub first, then ethics.* — Bertolt Brecht

*The officer of every corporation should feel in his heart — in his very soul — that he is responsible, not merely to make dividends for the stockholders of his company, but to enhance the general prosperity and the moral sentiment of the United States.* — Adolphus Green, whose expansive nature was encouraged by the near-monopoly status of his National Biscuit Company when he founded it in 1898

*Few trends could so thoroughly undermine the very foundation of our free society as the acceptance of a social responsibility [for companies] other than to make as much money for their stockholders as possible. This is a fundamentally subversive doctrine.* — Nobel laureate economist Milton Friedman, whose academic roost, the University of Chicago, was founded as an act of social responsibility by the pioneer pirate-philanthropist John D. Rockefeller

**correction** *n*. A decline in stock-market prices. Broker's response to clients: "Don't worry, the market was getting ahead of itself. Now that we've got this modest decline under our belts, prices are poised for a strategic recovery."

**correction, massive** *n*. A significant drop in stock-market prices. Broker's response: "Don't panic. By the way, we've been thinking about a strategic shift into T-bills."

**correction, massive, but the situation is fundamentally sound** *n*. A crash; i.e., October 1929, October 1987. Broker's response: "Kindly leave your name at the tone, and I'll get back to you the moment I find someone to hold my place in line here at the Varig ticket counter."

*It's like watching your mother-in-law go over the side of a cliff in your favorite car. It's a case of mixed emotions.* – Leonard Green, partner in leveraged buyout firm Gibbons Green van Amerongen, fearful at the sight of the October 1987 crash but also glad that stock prices were falling back to reasonable levels

**cost cutting** *n*. Reflex action in response to hard times, or the expected onset of same. In the mid-1980s, Citibank, the largest U.S. bank, exacted annual savings of $6,000 by lopping the word "Regards" off the ends of all Telex messages.

*Whenever I read about some company undertaking a cost-cutting program I know it's not a company that really knows what costs are all about. Spurts don't work in this area. The really good manager does not wake up in the morning and say, "This is the day I'm going to cut costs," any more than he wakes up and decides to practise breathing.* – Warren Buffett

**courage** *n.* A quality exhibited by the manager whose actions have proved successful. People who make tough decisions that don't work have not exhibited courage. They are exhibiting their resumes across town.

**crash** *n.* An inappropriate term. Use **correction**.

**crater** *v.* To flop, as in a deal that falls through. Common usage: "If we don't find a way maximize the optimizers, this deal's gonna crater on us."

**credit** *n.* 1. Debt, or the appearance of sufficient probity that bankers and suppliers will trust you with some. 2. Something employers receive in recognition of their employees' efforts.

*Authority provides a license to steal ideas, even in front of those who originated them ... A subordinate whose ideas are appropriated is expected to be a good sport about the matter; not to balk at so being used is one attribute of the good team player.* – Robert Jackall, *Moral Mazes*

**crisis management** *n.* The decision as to whether the CEO should be sent to the scene of the environmental disaster or shut up in his den, where his lack of knowledge and sensitivity has little shock value.

*Any idiot can face a crisis — it's this day-to-day living that wears you out.* — Anton Chekov

**critical mass** *n.* The point of no return.

**crown jewel** *n.* An asset whose Sirenic beauty inclines distant admirers not to observe the treacherous shoals about her feet.

*Many a man in love with a dimple makes the mistake of marrying the whole girl.* — Stephen Leacock

**dark night** *n.* In the entertainment industry, an evening in which a film played to empty seats. A common remedy for this problem is to **paper the house**.

**debt** *n.* A way of postponing until tomorrow obligations you cannot meet today.

*The Lord forbid that I should be out of debt, as if, indeed, I could not be trusted.* – Francis Rabelais

*You don't deserve to be called an entrepreneur unless you've mortgaged your house to the business.* – Ted Rogers, Canadian cable-TV czar

**decentralization** *n.* A shift of the onus for having to answer for mistakes from head office to the field.

**decision support** *n.* Advice and data selectively culled from peers and consultants to reinforce your loopy convictions.

**deficit financing** *n.* The act of purchasing something with sworn intentions rather than money.

*Ten years ago the deficit on my farm was about a hundred dollars; but by well-designed capital expenditure, by drainage and by greater attention to details, I have got it into the thousands.* – Stephen Leacock

**dehire** *v.* To terminate with extreme regret and, often, little else. (See **outplacement**)

**delegate** *v.* The generous act of allowing others to do the things you haven't time for or aren't any good at, freeing you to concentrate on taking the credit for their jobs well done.

*Conserve your time and energy because you never know when a crisis will arise that you will have to handle. Ronald Reagan is the ultimate recent practitioner of the conservation rule, although Calvin Coolidge had Reagan beat. Legend has it that the only two things Coolidge liked to have on his desk were his feet.* – Terry Eastland, senior civil servant in the Reagan administration

**deleverage** *v.* A massive sale of assets in order to shed unruly debt, followed by a bread-and-water diet.

*What epitomized the 1980s was, Spend now, pay later. What will epitomize the 1990s is, Pay now.* – David Colander, economics professor at Middlebury College

**demographics** *n.* The selective seduction of the economically correct – people with above-average education, income and propensity to spend – leaving the rest of us on the sidelines to watch in peace.

**depreciation** *n.* The periodic cost assigned to the reduction in value and usefulness of an asset. An example is the upgrading of golden parachutes for senior executives.

**desk** *n.* A trophy of war, the size of which indicates the full measure of its occupant's career accomplishment. (See **work surface**)

**devil's advocate, Let me play the** *phrase.* Translation: Not only is your idea stupid, it's safe to say so in front of all these people. By the way, your fly's open.

**difficult, It is** *phrase.* A Japanese expression meaning "no."

**digithead** *n.* A person who dismisses as unworthy any creative idea that cannot readily be expressed in mathematical formulae. (See **compusavant**)

**diminishing returns, law of** *n.* The formula by which fiscal authorities determine to what extent a hike in the rate of taxation will encourage a decline in citizens reporting their income. (See **Laffer curve**)

**director, outside** *n.* 1. A member of the board of directors who brings a fresh, unbiased perspective to its deliberations, given that he is not an employee of the firm and merely collects fat legal or consulting fees from the board's chairman and CEO. 2. A non-employee member of the board who, as a senior officer of one of the firm's major suppliers, is ideally suited to advise his colleagues on the selection of suppliers in his industry. 3. A non-employee director who is a senior administrator of a medical, academic or cultural institution and who, while not totally conversant with the firm's line of business, is ideally suited to the task of identifying worthy recipients of the firm's charitable donations.

**discontinued operations** *n*. Non-core assets or **dogs** that management has given up on, but which continue to clutter up the balance sheet until they can be closed or sold.

**disinflation** *n*. When more costs less, if only you had a job.

**dislocation** *n*. An unfortunate incident, such as the collapse of a company's markets or the national economy, requiring shutdowns, layoffs and the suspension of dividends. Announcements in this connection usually convey a certain unfortunate inevitability to the event – as in the dentist holding himself blameless but regretful about the "sensations" to follow.

**dis-optimal** *adj*. Not the best of situations, disastrous.

*Fiscal 1985 would have marked another year of gratifying progress had we not somehow managed to lose $570 million on a revenue base of $26.18. In that strict sense, the year was dis-optimal.* – fictional annual report summary, *The Globe and Mail*

**disposable income** *n*. A fiction of consumer spending power, which economists arrive at by subtracting income taxes and social insurance premiums from income. True disposable income is, of course, calculated by subtracting, in addition, property and sales taxes; union and professional association membership dues; alimony and child-support payments; home heating and repair expenses; car-related charges, including gasoline, parking and the replacement of the transmission, forward wheel assembly, all four tires, or equivalent; interest on outstanding credit card debts; admission tickets to rock concerts, zoos and theme parks purchased in the interest of maintaining domestic tranquillity; and the cost of at least one new outfit for the office. The balance, if positive, may be disposable. Certainly it is miraculous.

**diversification** *n.* Not having all your eggs in one basket. The choice not to be exposed to the vagaries of one industry, but rather to the vagaries of several, about which you know little or nothing. The realization of this folly, after the fact, prompts a restructuring or "strategic refocusing": the unloading of assets that have proved unmanageable, along with the massive debt accumulated in their purchase. (See **conglomerate** and **stick-to-your-knitting strategy**)

*There's a perception in this country that you're better off if you're in two lousy businesses than if you're in one good one.* – Robert C. Goizueta, chairman, Coca-Cola Co.

**divine right of capitalists** *n.* A doctrine which views with suspicion the notion that outsiders to business have any role in the stewardship of commercial enterprises.

*The rights and interests of the laboring men will be cared for, not by the labor union agitators, but by the Christian men to whom God in His infinite wisdom has given control of the property interests of the country.* – George F. Baer, head of the Reading Railroad, at the turn of the century

**dog** *n*. An asset that is a chronic money-loser and will soon be put up for adoption.

**dog and pony show** *n*. An entertainment for the young at heart, in which a CEO and his back-up band tour the country, previewing small gatherings of bankers and investment dealers with the tricks they will be able to perform with the funds the CEO hopes his audience will raise by selling large amounts of his stock.

**dog, doing the** *v*. A career strategy in which the candidate's advancement depends on his ability to teach dogs to stop playing dead.

*Barrett quickly zeroed in on a fast-track strategy: take the jobs the locals didn't want. Based on the premise that it was easier to make a mark by making something bad look good – or even slightly better – he asked to be transferred to the worst branches in the system ... After "doing" a couple of dog branches, his skills with people were recognized and he was invited to work in the personnel department*

*at head office. By 1978, at age 34, he had his first executive job.*
– Robert Collison, describing Matthew Barrett's early days at the Bank of Montreal, where he is now chairman and CEO, in *Canadian Business*

**dollar–cost averaging** *n*. A theory favored by brokers, in which the investor is invited to throw good money after bad by increasing his holding in a stock that has declined in value. In this way, the investor reduces the cost per share of his original investment. The alternative response, shooting the broker, would be illegal.

**downside risk** *n*. On the other hand, you could lose every penny you've invested. (See **upside potential**)

**downsize** *v*. A drastic scaling back of assets to the bare minimum, and also of expectations, which now can accurately be summarized with the word "survival." (See **streamline**)

*We sold off everything we could … It was like flying a plane, and you're tossing stuff out of the plane just trying to keep above the trees.* – Ted Rogers, cable-TV magnate, describing his response to an early-1980s brush with insolvency

**due diligence** *n*. The precaution, after watching a horse that jumps well, of examining its teeth before buying it.

**ear candy** *n.* A platitude tailored to a specific occasion. At the annual meeting, the CEO will remind shareholders of his sworn adherence to the pursuit of "wholly bottom-line objectives"; on a plant tour, he alludes to the connection between higher productivity and a "climate of enriched compensation"; and at a government inquiry he testifies his firm has an "uncompromising commitment to environmental enhancement." The term originates in the recording industry, in reference to catchy but vacuous pop tunes that earn instant, widespread appeal.

*Charm us, orator, till the lion look no larger than the cat.* – Alfred, Lord Tennyson

*You have to look at leadership through the eyes of followers. Lech Walesa told Congress that there is a declining world market for*

*words. He's right. The only thing the world believes is behavior, because we all see it instantaneously. None of us may preach anymore. We must behave.* – Max DePree, chairman and retired CEO of office furniture maker Herman Miller Inc., in *Fortune*

*Occasionally, words must serve to veil the facts. But this must happen in such a way that no one becomes aware of it; or, if it should be noticed, excuses must be at hand, to be produced immediately.* – Niccolo Machiavelli

**early retirement** *n.* A stress-related syndrome whose sufferers, drained by the rigors of the workday, pass the evenings by feeding the cat, reheating the remains of last night's Kraft Dinner and falling asleep during the second half of "thirty-something."

**earnings** *n*. Profits. The term, designed to cast the concept of profit in a more respectable light, came into widespread use in the 1950s, when the "profit motive" was under routine attack from postwar socialists.

**eccentric** *n*. An executive whose ideas are at marked variance to those of the corporate culture. Not a person to do lunch with.

**economics** *n*. A study of the incomprehensible with a view to rendering it unintelligible, happily with no impact on the subject.

*I think there are two areas where new ideas are terribly dangerous – economics and sex. By and large, it's all been tried before, and if it's new, it's probably illegal or dangerous or unhealthy.* – Felix Rohatyn, investment banker

**economies of scale** *n*. Theory that suggests a company should strive to increase volume in order to reduce unit price, putting aside the truism that the bigger the enterprise, the harder it falls.

**economist** *n*. A forecaster once commonly believed to have shamanistic powers before records were kept.

*An economist is a person who, when he finds something that works in practice, wonders if it will work in theory.* – Walter Heller, chief economic advisor to Presidents John Kennedy and Lyndon Johnson.

**ecopreneur** *n*. A person who derives his livelihood by mining veins of guilt.

**ecosystem** *n*. A corruption of the archaic term "ego-system," the delicately balanced system of life-forms that make up a company's managerial work force.

**elephant** *n*. A mouse built to government specifications.

**elephant-man strategy** *n*. A project which, on the face of it, is too frightening to adopt, no matter what promise it might hold for long-term benefits. Such proposals invariably alienate everyone because no one at the company has done anything like this before. Conversely, projects that promise misery in the long run can be successfully launched if sold as a pet project of the CEO; described as bursting with "synergy"; or are wildly beyond the company's financial or managerial capacity.

**entrepreneurialism, paper** *n*. A term coined by Harvard economist Robert Reich to describe the 1980s plague of hostile takeovers, tax ploys, accounting dodges and endless litigation that drained the economy of life and the schools of their best talent.

**environmental audit** *n.* How many trees did we kill today?

**environmental impact** *n.* An unanticipated, unwanted side effect of an industrial process. An obvious example is the near extinction of the purple zebra, whose skin is valued by the airline industry for seat coverings.

**equity émigré** *n.* A person who cashes in on the swiftly appreciating value of one house in order to plow the proceeds into another, much larger home in a more affordable locale. In the late 1980s, this trend was most noticeable in the executive exodus from southern California to Oregon and Washington and in southern Ontario – the two areas of North America with the fastest-rising house prices.

**erratic** *adj.* Term for the entrepreneur who comes up with a new project to bet the whole company on each time the firm threatens to record its first meaningful profit. Ted Turner stopped doing this in the mid-1980s. His current reputation as a **visionary** dates from this decision.

**error in judgment** *n.* A grievous mistake made by someone in authority.

**excess** *n.* An indulgence giving cause for egress, notably of payments in the service of debt.

*I have always done everything in excess. There are no limits – none whatsoever.* – Pierre Peladeau, whose experiments with tabloid newspaper publishing in Quebec and Philadelphia have sometimes lacked success, but never daring

**excursion** *n.* 1. A walk in the woods with the devil. 2. In the defense industries, the blueprints for a $500 hammer and a $3,000 toilet seat.

**exhibitionist** *n.* A tycoon who curtails speculation on the possibility of a complex personality by appearing on "Lifestyles of the Rich and Famous."

**exile package** *n.* Set of grimy misdemeanors – allegations of illicit use of company aircraft, for instance, and redeployment of corporate funds to a son-in-law's furniture-repair shop – fabricated as a prelude to the forced resignation of a high-level executive.

*It is not enough to kill an adversary. He must first be dishonored.* – Sergei Nechayev, nineteenth-century Russian revolutionary

**exit package** *n.* Here's your premature-retirement bonus. What's your hurry?

**exploding bonus** *n.* A signing bonus offered to college graduates that places a premium on greed, paying, say, a $20,000 bonus if the recruit signs right away, $16,000 if he waits a day, $12,000 the day after, and so on until the bonus "explodes," or disappears.

**exposure** *n.* The particular vulnerabilities of a particular business. The ski-resort operator lives in fear of unseasonable warm weather; the dentist is troubled by a drop-off in Twinkie sales; the running shoe merchant trembles at the exponential increase in couch potatoes.

**face** *n*. Visibility. Hard work is its own reward, provided everyone knows about it. You show your face at company gatherings to be interrogated about your remarkable skill and determination, and follow up with mildly self-flattering memos to the appropriate authorities.

**facilitating payment** *n*. A bribe. (See **speed money**)

*Too poor for a bribe, and too proud to importune,*
*He had not the method of making a fortune.* – Thomas Gray

**failure** *n*. The absence of success. (See **mistake**)

*Not failure, but low aim is crime.* – James Russell Lowell

*If a thing's worth doing, it is worth doing badly.* – G.K. Chesterton

*Allow me to offer my congratulations on the truly admirable skill you have shown in keeping clear of the mark. Not to have hit once in so many trials, argues the most splendid talents for missing.* — Thomas De Quincey

**fairness opinion** *n.* A document purporting to show the fair value of a company's shares at the moment when a related party, usually a controlling shareholder, is attempting to buy the shares from minority shareholders. Fairness opinions tend to be greeted with skepticism since they usually are commissioned by the company whose shares are being bought, whose board wants the shares to *be* bought. Moreover, the minority sees only the reported value of the shares, not the methodology for arriving at this figure.

**fallen angel** *n.* A derogatory term applied by brokers to a once highly touted stock in a transparent bid to distract investors from the brokers' own, no less apparent, plunge.

**family-friendly culture** *n.* A corporate workplace that is receptive to the idea of day-care facilities and flexible hours for workers with children, having already succeeded with the "spouses itinerary" at sales conferences.

*There is a person, it would appear, to whom the modern corporation is beginning to pay a good deal of attention … to wit, the wife.*

*"We control a man's environment in business and we lose it entirely when he crosses the threshold of his home," one executive says mournfully. "Management, therefore, has a challenge and an obligation to deliberately plan and create a favorable, constructive attitude on the part of the wife that will liberate her husband's total energies for the job." – Fortune, 1951*

**fate** *n.* The thing that takes over once you've done the best you can.

*I long ago came to the conclusion that all life is six to five against.* – Damon Runyan

*It is not true that life is one damn thing after another – it's one damn thing over and over.* – Edna St. Vincent Millay

**fault** *n.* The source of ignominy, whose location generally commands more attention than the search for restorative measures.

*Always acknowledge a fault frankly. This will throw those in authority off their guard and give you an opportunity to commit more.* – Mark Twain

**favorable market conditions** *n.* Dumb luck. Common usage: "Among favorable market conditions noted in the year past was an eight-month strike affecting our sole competitor, and a government decision making purchasers of our most profitable product eligible for a tax deduction."

**fear** *n.* A substitute for respect, and more easily inspired.

*Truth is in the eye of the beholden.* – Charles Revson

*When you have them by the balls, their hearts and minds will soon follow.* – sign on Charles Colson's wall when he was a top aide to President Richard Nixon

**financial gigolo** *n.* A prominent person recruited to lend prestige to a board of directors while posing no threat to management's control; coined in 1934 by William O. Douglas, future U.S. Supreme Court associate justice. Alexander Haig, former U.S. secretary of state, sat on the board of Allegheny International (Sunbeam appliances) at the time of its near-collapse; Gerald Ford served as a consultant of the failed Fidelity Trust Co. of Edmonton. (See **board of directors**)

**fine firm** *n.* In the securities industry, a compliment that is meant to wound.

*"Wasserstein Perella & Co., although a fine firm, is basically a one-product firm,"* [Kim Fennebresque of First Boston] told Investment Dealers Digest ... *Fennebresque knew the term* fine

firm *would rankle the Wasserstein contingent. "In investment banking," he explained, "that's like saying she doesn't sweat much for a fat girl."* – Bryan Burrough and John Helyar, *Barbarians at the Gate*: The Fall of RJR Nabisco

**firing line** *n.* The terminal remark of a career.

*Hey you. Lawyer. I'm talkin' to you.* – Peter Cohen, investment banker. There may have been other reasons for Cohen's ouster as CEO of Shearson Lehman Hutton in late 1989, but it probably was not a coincidence that *Barbarians at the Gate*, released at that time, revealed him as a self-important hothead during his failed attempt to perform a leveraged buyout on RJR Nabisco.

**flamboyant** *adj.* Media euphemism hinting at odd behavior of a business figure in his private life, the details of which have been withheld on the grounds of good taste and the laws concerning libel.

**flame–out** *n.* Mission abort. The sudden explosion of a high-energy career fueled by unrealistically high goals.

*If all else fails, immortality can always be assured by spectacular failure.* – John Kenneth Galbraith

**flat management structure** *n.* In the geometry of reporting systems, a preference for the horizontal line over the pyramid.

*A compact organization lets all of us spend time managing the business rather than managing each other.* – Warren Buffett

**flight to cash** *n.* A selling panic in which investors exchange the tomorrows of stock for the today of bank deposits.

**flight to value** *n.* Or, more appropriate, a "return to senses"; a decision by investors to dump speculative issues in favor of blue chips.

**flip** *v.* An investment variation on the hot potato. The trick is in not being caught holding a hot property the moment the market suddenly cools down.

*We must also consider mean those who buy from merchants in order to resell immediately, for they would make no profit without much outright lying.* – Cicero

*The secret of success in my business is to buy old junk, fix it up a little and unload it upon other fellows.* – Charles Yerkes, Chicago financier, for whom the famed Yerkes Observatory is named

**flying circus** *n*. A tour of operations by the CEO and his entourage of senior managers. The object of the exercise, apart from justifying the cost of maintaining a corporate jet, is to praise those men and women in the field who are bringing the vision of head office to life – and to terrorize the rest.

*[Flying circuses] are not intended to do serious inspections of facilities, despite ostentatious displays of white-glove scrutiny, but rather to give ritualistic endorsements of work performed by local management, some of which, in fact, is often stimulated by such occasions.* – Robert Jackall, *Moral Mazes*

**folkie** *n*. A person given to the use of popular expressions. Businesspeople tend to carry this off better than politicians. No one doubts that Sam Walton of Wal-Mart, America's richest man, likes the pickup truck he tools around in. During the 1988 presidential campaign, George Bush attempted to affect populist roots with mixed results. Asked at a truck stop if he would care for some coffee, Bush replied, "Er, yes – but just a splash."

**forecaster** *n.* Someone who tortures your imagination by predicting things that do not come to pass, and becalms it by failing to warn or convince you of things that do.

*Caesar: The ides of March are come.*
*Soothsayer: Ay, Caesar; but not gone.* – William Shakespeare

*Have you heard about the economist's version of Trivial Pursuit? Thirty questions and 300 correct answers.* – Fortune

*Predicting energy prices in recent years has become as dangerous as playing leapfrog with a unicorn.* – Arden Haynes, CEO of Imperial Oil Ltd.

**forward-looking manner, We will consider it in a** *phrase.* Japanese expression for "no."

**free agent** *n.* A person with highly portable job skills, whose loyalties are more to himself and his profession than to his employer. Short-term goals are of acute importance to the free agent, whose activities are geared more to impressing prospective future employers than the one that currently engages him.

**Friday night special** *n.* A financial statement or other corporate news release issued late Friday afternoon when reporters are scrambling to meet their deadlines, and are thus unable to question its contents too closely before rushing it into print. The device was pioneered by government for disclosing patronage appointments and pork-barrel contracts. It is always best to report poor financial results on a Friday. By Monday, the next publishing day, expressions of shock and indignation by investment analysts and other interested parties tend to be treated by editors and readers as old news.

**friend** *n.* An enemy with whom you have yet to do business.

*You learn in this business, if you want a friend, get a dog.* – Carl Icahn, takeover specialist

*To be successful in business, you need friends. To be very successful, you need enemies.* – Christopher Ondaatje, Toronto financier

**front office** *n.* 1. The place where the suits roost, final destination of aspiring, upwardly mobile managers. 2. The place from which stirring calls to action, harsh edicts to control costs and layoff notices flow.

**full disclosure** n. Not to be used. See **circumspection**

*If one tells the truth, one is sure, sooner or later, to be found out.* – Oscar Wilde

*If you have a mother-in-law with only one eye and she has it in the center of her forehead, you don't keep her in the living room.* — Lyndon Johnson, explaining why he kept public knowledge of the Vietnamese conflict to a minimum

**fully valued** *adj.* Sell. A euphemistic term employed by brokers to describe a stock whose price adequately reflects its investment potential, and is unlikely to rise further.

**fundamental analysis** *n.* One of the two principal schools of investment analysis. The other is technical analysis, which predicts share-price trends on the basis of numerical data, such as industry cycles and historical trading records. The fundamentalist takes a more basic approach. In making his assessment of a company's prospects, he notes the apparent lack of customers lining up for the company's products, the devastating fire that struck its central warehouse and the implications of the CEO's recent decision to conduct all business from a yacht in the Aegean.

**further study, This is a great idea, and it deserves** *phrase.* Translation: This proposal's so interesting I think everyone should see it. So I'm having it fashioned into placemats for the employee cafeteria.

# $\mathcal{G}$

**GAAP** *n.* Generally accepted accounting principles. The rare acronym that has more meaning than the words it stands for. (See **auditor's report**)

**gadfly** *n.* A professional crank shareholder who drags out annual meetings by peppering management with silly questions while other shareholders twitch restlessly, waiting for the coffee and muffins.

*No. And at the directors' meeting this morning, we voted that you could ask that question of only one director.* – Donald Graham, publisher of *The Washington Post*, responding to a shareholder's question at Washington Post Co.'s annual meeting: "Have you ever committed adultery?"

**gender revenge** *n.* The coming triumph of women in the workplace.

*When the day comes that American Express Co. has to hire a female employee, it will close its doors.* – James Congdell Fargo, AmEx president from 1881 to 1914

*Companies farsighted enough to see the labor shortages looming are already doing things to attract and keep good women. In the 1990s women should have more bargaining power than they have ever had.* – Betty Friedan, author of *The Feminine Mystique*, in *Fortune*

*To retain those [women] who opt out of corporate life, we clearly need benefits like day care and spousal relocation, but there should be more. Clothing allowances, for example. It costs a woman, in my estimate, two or three times as much as a man to dress for the executive workplace. Or – try this on your human resource people – a "hassle bonus." Having children while maintaining a job is one hell of a hassle. How about a $10,000 annual bonus for a woman between the ages of 35 and 45? It would vest after 10*

*years, when she would get $100,000 plus any capital apprecia-*
*tion – a good start toward educating those children.* – Stephen
A. Garrison, CEO of executive search firm Ward Howell
International, in *Fortune*

**gigadeal** *n.* A big deal. In its essentials, a deal is a deal is a
deal – the principles are always the same. But no one notices
a garden-variety deal; and a megadeal barely rates attention.
A gigadeal is worth $28 billion (the record-setting LBO
takeover of RJR Nabisco in 1989).

**glamor stock** *n.* Shares in the hula-hoop and cold-fusion
companies that *Business Week* claims everyone is buying.

**glass ceiling** *n.* A transparent but effective shield protecting
the fairer sex from exposure to the rigors of senior-level mis-
management.

**glitzkrieg** *n.* Term coined by *Newsweek* for rampant com-
mercialism associated with the one-hundredth anniversary of
Statue of Liberty in 1986.

**God** *n.* An unwitting ally in many corporate endeavors.

*The rich man is the moral man. Godliness is in league with riches.*
– William Laurence, Episcopal bishop, preaching in the late

1800s to his wealthy New York congregation, among whom was counted J. Pierpont Morgan

*I think God is using this company as a vehicle. I'm trying to take the beautiful creatures He created and help them reach down within themselves to bring out all the ability He gave them.* – Mary Kay Ash, founder of Mary Kay Cosmetics

*Would we be sacrilegious if we were to call You the First Great Entrepreneur? Your computer disks are chock-full of wisdom available to us if we will study the program and ... consider the readouts.* – Louis H. Evans Jr., of the National Presbyterian Church, invoking the Almighty in a prayer to open a White House conference on small business in 1986

**gold** *n.* In some cultures, an effective proxy for love.

*Gold. If you love her enough.* – ad slogan of jewelry marketer International Gold Corp. Ltd.

**gold–collar employee** *n.* An employee who knows which buttons to push to keep the company's wheels turning, and whose loyalty to the firm is secured with a generous compensation package. (See **free agent**)

**golden coffin** *n.* Sizable bequest by a company to the pet charity of its founder or long-time CEO upon his death:

coined when Occidental Petroleum unveiled plans to donate to founder Armand Hammer's namesake foundation seven times his annual salary upon his death.

**golden handcuffs** *n.* Also called "golden cuff links." An exceedingly generous pay and benefits package designed to prevent an employee from defecting. Not to be confused with a golden handshake, an exceedingly generous wad of go-away money paid to an executive no longer wanted at the firm.

**gray market** *n.* The market for goods and services aimed at older consumers, which will take off when the baby boomers enter their golden years. The dawn of this era will be signaled by the emergence of Brian Wilson as a spokesperson for retirement annuities, and the decision by McDonald's to convert its indoor playgrounds into euchre corners.

**grazing** *n.* Indiscriminate accumulation of acquisitions. (See **conglomerate**)

*Never eat more than you can lift.* – Miss Piggy

**greater fool theory** *n.* A rule of investing which holds that no matter how inflated the price of an investment, someone with an even less firm grip on reality can be found to take it off one's hands at a still higher price. The rule finds its most widespread application in the waning hours of a bull market.

*For a dear bargain is always annoying, particularly on this account, that it is a reflection on the judgment of the buyer.* – Pliny the Younger

**greed** *n.* The defining ethic of the 1980s, a decade in which a record 100,000 Americans became millionaires each year.

*There are not many of us who remain sober when they have the opportunity to grow wealthy. The great multitude of men are of a clear contrary temper: what they desire they desire out of all measure; when they have the option of making a reasonable profit, they prefer to make an exorbitant one. This is why all classes of retailers, businessmen, tavern keepers are so unpopular and under so severe a social stigma.* – Plato, *Laws*

*Greed has been severely underestimated and denigrated. There is nothing wrong with avarice as a motive, as long as it doesn't lead to antisocial conduct.* – Conrad Black, Anglo-Canadian press magnate

**green** *n.* 1. The color of ambition; the light at the end of Daisy Buchanan's dock. 2. An environmental protection zealot. 3. A shade that until recently was thought by marketers to be a turnoff for consumers – hence the traditional avoidance of green packaging.

**green–friendly** *adj*. A product that enhances the environment or reduces the harm inflicted on the environment; or one that is sold on the basis that it does one of those two things, pending further research.

**greenmail** *n*. An anti-takeover measure, in which the target of a potential takeover buys back its own shares from a raider that has been accumulating its stock. The greenmail victim is required to buy the shares at a stiff premium, and often must borrow heavily to fund the purchase.

**greenophile** *n*. An executive who can bear being in the same room as the **greens** and affects their language, if not their dress code. While probably not wholly sympathetic to their point of view, the greenophile is less inclined than his corporate peers to denounce greens as "ecological fascists." Greenophiles are increasingly valued at energy, mining, chemical and forest-products firms, in the newly created post of Vice-President, Environment. A lonely individual, the greenophile is viewed as subversive within the firm, and as a window-dressing hypocrite outside of it.

**greenwashing** *n*. Money laundering on behalf of the drug trade, carried out by "smurfs." These teenagers and little old ladies show up at the teller's window to deposit a Safeway bag filled with $262,000 in five-dollar bills. The unusual nature of these transactions failed to make an impression on banks until recent laws forced financial institutions to inquire into the source of such funds.

**groin pull** *n.* An overexertion of machismo that alienates the colleagues from whom one is attempting to bully approval for a proposal. (See **laughter curve**)

**growth, negative** *n.* The incredible shrinking company or economy.

**growth stock** *n.* An investment whose badge of honor is that it does not pay a dividend; the profits are all reinvested in the business. The purpose of such a stock is, as Alfred Lord Tennyson wrote in a different context, "to strive, to seek, to find, and not to **yield**."

**gun belt** *n.* The U.S. defense industry.

**guru** *n.* A prominent economist or management consultant whose credentials have been established on the corporate lecture circuit and in the bookstores, and whose savantry is all the more remarkable given that he has never piloted a national economy or a corporation.

*A sign of celebrity is often that his name is worth more than his services.* – Daniel Boorstin

**headcount, We must absorb growth within the present** *phrase.* (See **attrition** and **horizontal career path**)

**hero** *n.* A manager whose triumphs obscure the memory of his mistakes. (See **bum**)

**high moral ground** *n.* Purported terra nova of the enlightened 1990s manager, who will need the agility of a Sherpa to traverse it.

**historical romance** *n.* A five-year statement of corporate earnings, skillfully adjusted to satisfy investors' expectations of a happy ending.

*Others may fear what the morrow may bring, but I am afraid of what happened yesterday.* – Old Arab saying

**hold** *v.* What the broker suggests you do with one of your ailing stocks when what he means is that you should sell. He'd like to tell you to sell, but his colleagues in the underwriting department are trying at this very moment to unload a new issue of that same ailing company's stock. (See **Chinese wall**)

**holding company** *n.* A shell which, when cracked open, produces a puff of dust and the address of a post-office box in Panama City.

*A holding company is a thing where you hand an accomplice the goods while the policeman searches you.* – Will Rogers

**honesty** *n.* A last resort when the usual avenues fail.

*For the merchant, even honesty is a financial speculation.* – Charles-Pierre Baudelaire

*Lord, help me to be pure, but not yet.* – St. Augustine

**horizontal career path** *n.* At a recession-racked firm, an elaborate motivation program consisting of lateral moves, days off, secondments, training sessions and special awards offered in place of the old and somewhat more satisfying regimen of promotions, raises and bonuses.

**HR** *n.* 1. New term for the no longer fashionable "human resources," itself a replacement for the distinctly unfashionable "personnel." 2. Heads roll.

**humidifier effect** *n.* An adverse health condition affecting workers in office towers with sealed windows. Symptoms include headaches, lethargy, eye irritation and other side effects of breathing stale air.

**Icarus factor** *n.* An affliction that causes the manager, too readily convinced of his abilities and potential for upward mobility, to seek for himself a grandiose project that proves his undoing – a process that finds its culmination, more often than not, in the resolute indifference to his cries for help among peers whose good nature he would have done better to cultivate. In the case of arrogant institutions, the operative term is Drexel factor.

**immediately** *adv.* In the large organization, "tomorrow" or, failing that, within the next few months. But *now*, be warned, means "now."

**immunization, portfolio** *n.* The periodic administration of a booster shot to guard against viral fecklessness. In currency trading, for instance, the purchase of options on other currencies sure to rise if one already held should fall; and the taking of night courses in turret-lathe operation as a precaution in case the above precaution fails.

**implications, That's a good idea, but there are a number of** *phrase.* Translation: No. Come back when you've done your homework.

**impressionistic economics** *n.* A system of forecasting modeled on the weatherman who looks out the window rather than studying a chart. The impressionist is concerned with the availability of parking spaces at the shopping mall or flights to a popular sun spot, and with the decision by retailers to start Christmas sales in August. (See **tailgating factor**)

**indignant** *adj.* Term that draws its meaning from the sayings of Conrad Black, Anglo-Canadian press baron. Characteristic expression: "I am amazed by the number of so-called financial experts who are luxuriating in the view that I am some sort of punch-drunk prizefighter on the ropes. Well, screw them."

**inflation** *n.* When less costs more.

**infostructure** *n.* Formerly the mail room. The electronically assisted system of people, computers, fax machines, voice mail and cellular phones by which managers receive and misinterpret information.

**inheritance** *n.* The reward for selecting successful parents.

*Saving is a very fine thing, especially when your parents have done it for you.* – Winston Churchill

*Inherited wealth ... is certain death to ambition as cocaine is to morality.* – William Vanderbilt, grandson and heir to the fortune of Cornelius Vanderbilt

*My rise to the top was through sheer ability and inheritance.* – Malcolm Forbes

**inscrutable** *adj.* Term commonly applied to a financier whose methods are not yet clearly understood by the world outside the Securities and Exchange Commission.

**institutional imperative** *n.* The power of ennui.

*In business school, I was given no hint of the imperative's existence ... I thought then that decent, intelligent, and experienced managers would automatically make rational business decisions. But I learned over time that isn't so ... For example: (1) As if gov-*

erned by Newton's first law of motion, an institution will resist any change in its current direction; (2) Just as work expands to fill available time, corporate projects or acquisitions will materialize to soak up available funds; (3) Any business craving of the leader, however foolish, will be quickly supported by detailed rate-of-return and strategic studies prepared by his troops; and (4) The behavior of peer companies, whether they are expanding, acquiring, setting compensation, or whatever, will be mindlessly imitated. Institutional dynamics, not venality or stupidity, set business on these courses, which are too often misguided. – Warren Buffett

**integrity** *n.* A reputation for doing the right thing even when no one's looking.

*The louder he talked of his honor, the faster we counted our spoons.* – Ralph Waldo Emerson

**interests, Left to pursue other** *phrase.* Exit line. Translation: No longer wanted at the firm.

**Internal Revenue Service** *n.* The least forgiving silent partner.

*Some of them are afraid of terrorists – you know, the IRS.* – Malcolm Forbes, explaining why some tycoons seek to avoid mention in the annual *Forbes 400* list of America's wealthiest people.

**intrapreneur** *n.* Nickname for inventor Arthur Fry, of 3M Corp., who on company time came up with the famed Post-it notes as a way to mark his place in a hymnal. It was hoped that this experiment in entrepreneurialism within a large organization would take hold elsewhere. It was abandoned, however, in favor of studies in leveraged buyouts.

**investment analyst** *n.* A spectator of apparent saintly disposition, who, having opted not to amass a fortune by devoting his own funds to the market, imparts his knowledge to untutored devotees whom he counsels to take the plunge. From time to time, the analyst issues reports which scathingly prod managers of great enterprises to do better – lest the analyst's clients mistake the casual stewardship of those firms with his own less than nimble judgment in touting their shares. The rule of his trade is: Those who can, do; those who can't, recommend.

*A CEO may be a fool and fail to know it, but not if the shares of his company are publicly traded.* – Katherine Westcott

*Just as a stopped clock has the correct time twice a day, so even the lousiest analyst can claim a superior track record.* – Forbes

**investment cycle** *n.* The roughly predictable pattern in which a period when investors are losing a lot of money ends, and a new one begins in which investors lose much larger amounts.

*October is one of the peculiarly dangerous months to speculate in stocks. The others are July, January, September, April, November, May, March, June, December, August and February.* – Mark Twain

**investment grade** *adj.* Term for a financial instrument of sturdy repute. Unlike the prospects in the seventh race at Meadowlands, it often comes with an attractive certificate to remind you of its provenance.

**investment opportunity** *n.* Shares in that plastic wind-up koala bear import-export firm that your broker is so keen for you to buy. Sometimes known as a "ground-floor opportunity," in which case you may have difficulty locating the firm's name in the phone book.

# 𝒥

**Japlash** *n.* Xenophobic reaction to the Japanese acquisition of American industrial icons, including Rockefeller Center, Columbia Pictures, the U.S. car buyer and Cyndi Lauper.

*Comedian Jay Leno says the new Japanese luxury car, Lexus, is having some recall problems. Seems there are three conditions they must work on:*
- *The cruise control will sometimes not shut off.*
- *The center brake light may melt.*
- *It seems to make sudden stops in front of all U.S. real estate offices. – The Globe and Mail, 1989*

**Japlish** *n.* New Japanese vocabulary consisting of Western business terms, such as "chekku" (check or cheque), "majin" (profit margin), "pii aru" (p-ublic r-elations) and "dinosaur" (General Motors).

**Japspeak** *n.* A language that derives its power from the use of deceptively deferential phrases.

*Our expressions are very inadequate … It's very difficult for us to speak directly. We use a kind of code. For example:* I will consider it. *For us, this means:* No. *Faced with this kind of inability to communicate, we have to worry about becoming isolated in the next decade.* – Reiichi Yumikura, president of the Japanese textile and chemical giant Asahi Chemical Industry, exhibiting the traditional Japanese gift for describing a blessing as a curse

**Jennifer syndrome** *n.* The propensity of tycoons to impress their second, younger wives with displays of macho acquisitiveness as a sign of undiminished virility. (See **trophy wife**)

*[Charles Hugel, chairman of RJR Nabisco, had been married to the same woman for thirty-six years, and he wondered whether the changes he saw in [Ross] Johnson could be attributed to [Johnson's wife] Laurie. The phenomenon of rich, older men taking pretty, young, second wives has been called the Jennifer Syndrome, and Hugel was the kind of solid citizen who thought older husbands often did foolish things to show off for their Jennifers. He felt that ambitious women such as Laurie Johnson, Susan Gutfreund, Linda Robinson, and Carolyne Roehm – in New York they called them "trophy wives" – compared notes on how their new husbands were doing, egging them on to grandeur.* – Bryan Burrough and John Helyar, *Barbarians at the Gate: The Fall of RJR Nabisco*

**junk bomb** *n*. A junk bond set to explode in the investor's portfolio when bankruptcy overtakes the firm that issued it.

**junk bond** *n*. A bond which pays an unusually high rate of interest to compensate for the low credit rating of the issuer. Junk bond pioneer Michael Milken, who fueled an epidemic of junk-financed takeovers in the 1980s, preferred the term "high-yield securities." Holders of high-yield securities in the bankrupt Allied-Federated Stores, Revco DS and other failed leveraged buyouts prefer the term "junk."

**jury proof** *v*. Careful preparation of a corporate document to ensure that it can withstand the most detailed scrutiny. In particular, the effort taken by a company, when issuing new shares, to ensure that the prospectus leaves no doubt as to the dizzying investment potential of the shares and probity of the party issuing them.

**just–in–time** *n.* The insistence that raw materials be shipped just in time for use, in order that suppliers pay the penalty for a manufacturer's miscalculations.

**Laffer curve** *n*. An economic model that plots the tax rate against the taxes actually collected. As the rate rises, there inevitably comes a point where revenues stop rising and begin to fall, as oppressed taxpayers indulge in creative tax dodges or fail to report all their income.

*The art of taxation consists in so plucking the goose as to obtain the largest amount of feathers with the least amount of hissing.* – Jean-Baptiste Colbert

**laughter curve** *n*. The trajectory by which an executive reaches the point during a presentation when his or her proposal has attracted so much ridicule that it is pointless to continue.

**lawyer** *n*. A specialist who renders legal that which the company has already done.

*There's a lot of things these old boys have done that are within the law, but it's so near the edge you couldn't slip a razor between their acts and a prosecution.* – Will Rogers

*Gentlemen:*
*You have undertaken to cheat me. I won't sue you, for the law is too slow. I'll ruin you.*
*Yours truly,*
*Cornelius Vanderbilt*

**layoff** *n.* An act of contrition in which senior management offers up the bodies of lesser employees as atonement for its misjudgments.

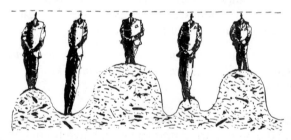

**level playing field** *n.* A competitive arena in which no player has an unfair advantage. The perfect level playing field (known as a monopoly) is obtained when the field has been purged of all but one player.

**leverage** *n.* The act of borrowing five cents to purchase control of something worth one dollar in the expectation of locating someone with five dollars to unload it upon.

**leveraged buyout (LBO)** *n.* A corporate takeover in which all or most of the target's cash and assets are used to finance its own takeover by another firm. Managers of the LBO'd firm find that the onerous task of planning for plant improvements and research and development has been lifted from their shoulders, as the firm no longer has funds for either activity.

*You need less money to open a shoeshine shop than you do to buy a $2 billion company; let's be honest about it. But to buy a shoeshine store, if it costs $3,000, you need $3,000. If you don't got it in cash, you need to bring it by Thursday. But if it's an LBO, not only do you not have to bring it, you don't have to see it, you don't know where you're going to get it, nobody knows where they got it from.* – Jackie Mason, "What the Hell is an LBO?"

**levity** *n.* The soul of grit.

*Overnight the corporate culture was transformed into a facsimile of Johnson's flip, breezy manner. Now when Standard Brands managers met, the sessions were laced with outrageous profanity and raucous challenges. "All right," Johnson liked to convene problem-solving meetings, "whose cock is on the anvil on this one?"* – authors Bryan Burrough and John Helyar, describing the regime of F. Ross Johnson as CEO of Standard Brands (now part of RJR Nabisco), in *Barbarians at the Gate*

**life, get a** *phrase.* Popular expression to silence bean-counters and other meddlesome individuals who have nothing better to do than nitpick.

**limited liability** *n.* The entrepreneur's house, which he has had the good sense to register in a loved one's name. If the loved one is a spouse, the entrepreneur will ensure that a prenuptual agreement covers the important aspects of "limited giveaway."

**liquidity** *n.* Sufficient cash to cover normal business requirements and unforeseen emergencies. Once a fundamental requirement of doing business, an effort has been made to suspend this rule in the field of leveraged buyouts.

*Cash is virtue.* – Lord Byron

**litigation support** *n.* The private eyes, forensic accountants and professional witnesses who assist your lawyer in bringing virtue to your cause and wealth to theirs.

**lobbyist** *n.* A person paid to advance a company's cause through sweet reason and gentle persuasion on government – several times a day, if necessary; on yachts and at hunting resorts, if possible.

*Question: Why are there more flies in Cairo than lobbyists in Washington? Answer: Cairo got first choice.* – Norman R. Augustine, CEO of Martin Marietta, *Augustine's Laws*

**lobby-lock** *n.* Congestion of lobbyists in Washington to the extent that few, if any, of their goals are reached, because they're all pushing and pulling in so many directions as to confuse legislators.

**lobbyspeak** *n.* The language that lobbyists inflict on legislators and regulators, highly flavored by self-interested pleas weakly disguised as calls to public service.

*"We're for competition, but ..." means, "You can pretty much disregard everything I've said up until now; start listening." "We are in favor of the shift in policy but we need a transition" means, "Your proposed decision should not go into effect until just somewhat after my lifetime." And, "All we are seeking is a level playing field" means, "Gimme, gimme."* – Mark Fowler, former chairman of the Federal Communications Commission

**loss** *n.* The Second Coming of a miscalculation.

**loyalty** *n.* Faith in the Supreme Company, based on its supposed resemblance to a kind uncle.

**lunch sometime, Let's have** *phrase.* Translation: Get lost. The expression "We should do business sometime" is equally dismissive, being freely adapted from the unrequited romance brush-off "I'll call you"– which means: With any luck you'll fall into the canal before guilt induces me to do so.

**management** *n.* The art of misdirection.

*So much of what we call management consists in making it difficult for people to work.* – Peter Drucker

*Take a 33-year-old man who assembles chairs. He's been doing it several years. He has a wife and two children. He knows what to do when the children have earaches, and how to get them through school. He probably serves on a volunteer board. And when he*

*comes to work we give him a supervisor. He doesn't need one. His*
*problem isn't to be supervised, it's to continue toward reaching his*
*potential.* – Max DePree, chairman and retired CEO of office
furniture maker Herman Miller Inc., in *Fortune*

**management by walking around** *n.* The practice of a
CEO who, while expanding his ambit of mischief, proves he
could not possibly have come up through the ranks.

*If you want a thing done, go – if not, send.* – Benjamin Franklin

**management depth, I like your idea, we just have to
make sure that it's executed with a sufficient amount
of** *phrase.* Translation: Yes. But you're not the one to run
with it.

**market share** *n.* The portion of the total market that a
company is able to obtain with its products. There are three
ways to obtain market share: 1. Work hard to create a
market where none existed by inventing a product that customers want. 2. Work hard to take market share away from
a competitor by offering better value than he does. 3. Buy
the competitor. Work hard to come up with a catchy name
for the combined enterprise.

*The meek shall inherit the world, but they'll never increase market
share.* – William McGowan, chairman of MCI Communications

*The soft drink industry in the 1980s tended toward the mindless pursuit of market share. Managing share without profit is like breathing air without oxygen. It feels okay for a while, but in the end it kills you.* – Roger Enrico, CEO of PepsiCo Worldwide Beverages, in *Fortune*

**marketing** *n.* A decision against letting the product speak for itself, recognizing that it may not be the most credible spokesman.

*He was a strange man. He wasn't very good at it.* – Charles Allsopp, an auctioneer at Christie's, explaining how Vincent van Gogh's *Sunflowers* – which sold at auction in 1987 for $39.9 million – was considered worthless when painted

**MBA** *n.* An academic degree held by bankers who specialize in Third World overlending. The letters stand for Mexico, Brazil and Argentina.

**MBO** *n.* Management buyout, or "My Boss Owns."

**McJob** *n.* A low-paying position in the service economy, unskilled except for learning to smile on the job.

*A McDonald's outlet is a machine that produces, with the help of unskilled machine attendants, a highly polished product. Through painstaking attention to total design and facilities planning, every-*

*thing is built integrally into the technology of the system. The only choice open to the attendant is to operate it exactly as the designers intended.* – George Cohon, president of McDonald's Restaurants of Canada Ltd.

**mechanical, gone** *phrase.* Bane of the frequent flier. Common usage: "This is your captain speaking. Our takeoff will be delayed until we make a minor adjustment to the tail rudder and correct a short in the smoke-detector system in the forward loo. I'm afraid we've gone mechanical."

**meeting** *n.* 1. Man's most effective tool for preventing outbreaks of decisive action. 2. A means of sabotaging a project by killing it with critique. 3. A gathering called by an individual who wishes to invite contrary opinions to his position in order to "democratize," and thereby enforce, a decision he has no intention of modifying.

**megababble** *n.* Term coined by *Time* in the late 1980s to describe the upbeat gibberish of best-selling futurists such as John Naisbitt, a failed business consultant, who emerged from personal bankruptcy to enthrall readers with *Megatrends* and *Megatrends 2000.*

*I attend to the business of others, having lost my own.* – Horace

**Melpew** *n.* The language of the service economy.

*[At] McDonald's ... jaded 16 year olds stuff hamburgers into plastic containers or greet customers with a "virtually programmed" set of responses that, at least at the franchise I frequent, have evolved into a sort of slurred McSpeak. The universal greeting, "Melpew," a contraction of "May I help you?" may one day make the Oxford English Dictionary.* – Mickey Kaus, *The New York Times Book Review*

**memo** *n.* An effective device for avoiding clear and candid communication.

**memoir** *n.* Favored make-work project of retired tycoons; favored marketing effort of those still in office.

*The CEO memoir was a hot acquisition for a publisher in the wake of* Iacocca, *but they aren't so hot anymore. All these guys think their story is as colorful, interesting and unassailable as his was, but it's rarely true.* – Stuart Applebaum, a vice-president at Bantam Books, in 1987

**mentor** *n.* An individual who thoughtfully undertakes to advance your career on the tacit understanding that you, under no circumstances, will ever impede his.

**mingles** *n.* The family unit of the 1990s: single, unrelated people who buy a home together.

**missing in action** *n.* Fate of senior executives, often pretenders to the CEO, who run afoul of that individual in the course of proving themselves worthy to replace him, and leave of their own accord or are placed on "special assignment."

**mistake** *n.* The mother of humility, save in those instances where you have not been found out.

*There is no mistake; there has been no mistake; and there shall be no mistake.* – Arthur Wellesley, 1st Duke of Wellington

*Once the corporate ethos is that the corporation cannot have made a mistake, then it's going to go farther and farther off course. The CEO becomes a bit like a pilot in an aircraft who says to the altimeter, "What's the height?" and hears the altimeter reply, "What would you like it to be?"* – John Cleese, cofounder of "Monty Python's Flying Circus," now a producer of training films for business

*I'm the first to admit that our timing couldn't have been worse. But I take comfort in one fact: the last guy who was perfect in this world was crucified 2,000 years ago, too.* – Cedric Ritchie, CEO of the Bank of Nova Scotia, commenting on the bank's purchase of investment dealer McLeod Young Weir Ltd. shortly after the October 1987 stock-market crash

**mokatte makka** *phrase*. Traditional greeting in Osaka, Japan. Translation: Are you making a profit?

**money** *n*. The root of all.

*Money brings some happiness. But after a certain point, it just brings more money.* – Neil Simon

*Make money and the whole nation will conspire to call you a gentleman.* – Robert (Bob) Edwards, *Calgary Eye-Opener*

**multinational** *n*. A firm which, having established a footing in its homeland, has elected to push its luck overseas.

*I don't believe you can run a major U.S. company from abroad. George III tried to run the United States from Britain, and look what happened to him.* – Sir Gordon White, chairman of Hanson Industries Inc.

**multiple** *n*. The relation of a stock's price to the earnings of the firm that issued it. Under normal circumstances, a stock will trade in the range of five to fifteen times the firm's earnings per share. A multiple in the Fahrenheit freezing point range indicates a somewhat overheated stock. A multiple that approaches room temperature most likely has the word "technology" in its name.

**mushroom** *v.* The practice of transferring an underperforming executive to a dark, quiet place where he can do no more damage.

**mutual nonaggression pact** *n.* An old political adage updated for the corporate world, in which one warring executive promises to stop lying about the other if the other stops spreading the truth about him.

**muzzle clause** *n.* A bribe accepted by the prematurely retiring executive to ensure his circumspection regarding the embarrassing details giving rise to his departure. Typically, the generosity of an ex-executive's severance pay relates directly to his ability to keep his trap shut. The most exorbitant gag order on record was applied to H. Ross Perot, a former director and outspoken critic of General Motors. In 1986, G.M. agreed to buy back Perot's stock in the company for $700 million in an agreement that was intended to contractually silence him. It didn't. The very day the agreement was signed, Perot held a press conference at which he renewed his verbal assault on the perceived shortcomings of G.M. management.

**naked to your enemies** *adj.* A condition that arises when your mentor in the organization manages to get himself fired. In such circumstances, identifying a replacement personal apologist high in the corporate ranks is Job One.

**networking** *n.* The act of substituting career-advancement banter for conversation. Plebs seeking to develop a network of useful contacts join industry associations where they meet only other people with the same idea. Vice-presidents with executive vice-presidential aspirations strive for "presence" and an aura of upward mobility by "schmoozing" at gallery openings, regattas and political fetes. The truly powerful, meanwhile, enjoy blissful isolation on the back nine at Burning Tree, where the waiting list for new members is a thousand years long.

**nice-to-haves (NTH)** *n.* Frills, whose death knell is sounded with the gratuitous acknowledgment of their utility. By managing to appear at least mildly regretful about wielding the shears, the corporate Grim Trimmer is able to cut even the most sacrosanct items down to size. Common usage: "Listen, no one's knocking free meals, but a subsidized employee cafeteria is one of those nice-to-haves we just can't afford during a recession. I hate to say it, but I'm beginning to feel the same way about our R&D budget."

**Ninety-nine percent accuracy syndrome** *n.* The mistaken belief that 99 percent is a close enough approximation of perfection.

*We all believe no one can be perfect. Ninety-nine percent is good enough, right? What 99 percent accuracy really means is that for 15 minutes every day, your lights and refrigerator, your stove and telephone, would shut down. It means that two passengers on every air flight would reach their destinations minus their luggage. And it means that every year, 28 glowing sets of parents would cart the wrong baby home from the hospital.* – Conference Board of Canada report

**no–brainer** *n.* A correct decision that even a highly trained executive could hardly fail to make.

*Time will tell whether I have the qualities for this job. But I've been in banking 27 years, and you can teach a monkey any business after 27 years. After all, it's not brain surgery.* – Matthew Barrett, chairman and CEO, Bank of Montreal

**nuisance index** *n.* Measurement of price increases in everyday items, created by New York economist Irwin Kellner in 1986. At a time of near nonexistent inflation in the economy as a whole, Kellner's first index identified a 7 percent increase in the price of rye whiskey, an 18 percent hike in haircut prices, and a whopping 33 percent jump in the fee banks charge to process phone and utility bills. Conclusion: Makers of items bearing small price tags find the temptation to force a big, but likely unnoticed, price hike irresistible.

**off-agenda** *adj.* 1. An item raised at a meeting that catches the participants by surprise, thus easing or complicating its passage, depending on the timidity or backbone of those present. 2. In the larger sense, any development – usually a crisis or scandal – that distracts the leaders of an enterprise or government from pursuing their stated goals.

**off-balance sheet financing** *n.* A device for borrowing money without appearing to do so, usually by means of quietly setting up a separate entity to do the borrowing. Popular with business and governments during periods when balance sheets are being closely monitored by outsiders for adherence to self-proclaimed policies of budgetary restraint.

**opportunity cost** *n*. The time or money that could have been better spent doing something else. The opportunity cost for upwardly mobile individuals includes recreational reading, getting to know one's family and clothing that is not featured in the company's annual report.

**opportunity for learning** *phrase*. The bright side of a mistake.

**outplacement** *n*. Here's your resume-preparation advisor, what's your hurry?

**Pablumatic** *adj.* Mushy and taste-free, as in a corporate statement or report that adds to no one's knowledge and to everyone's confusion, but goes down easily.

**Pac Man defense** *n.* An anti-takeover tactic in which the target company retaliates with an offer to take over the firm seeking to buy *it*.

**painting the tape** *n.* An illegal tactic among stock-market manipulators, in which large orders are broken into smaller ones in order to create the appearance of heavy buying. If successfully executed, this illusion of excited buying activity lures gullible investors into the action; the manipulators profit by selling out during the ensuing price escalation.

**panicity** *n*. A response to crises characterized by chaotic and superheated activity.

*What you have here is an Administration that has set its hair on fire and is trying to put it out with a hammer.* – Senator Alfonse D'Amato

**paper** *n*. The memo or other document that spells out your proposal, covers your behind or exposes your enemies to ridicule. Even the most persuasive orator knows enough to follow up with good paper.

**paper architecture** *n*. An elaborate project that never gets past the blueprint stage for lack of feasibility or money. Commonly a Byzantine network of far-flung business units and intricate reporting systems that, however hoary and venerable, has yet to generate more than a whisper of profit.

*Perfection of means and confusion of goals seem, in my opinion, to characterize our age.* – Albert Einstein

**paper the house** *v*. In the entertainment business, to give tickets away in order to create the impression of a full theater.

**paper trail** *n*. (See **audit trail**)

**parachute, Formica** *n.* Unemployment insurance.

**parachute, golden** *n.* Handsome severance payment, usually amounting to between three and five years' salary, for top executives of a company upon their dismissal or resignation from the firm. Often hastily put in place by besieged managements facing a hostile takeover.

*When I was running IBM, I was driven strongly by the fear of failure, fear of being counted out as a son trying to follow a father. Fight in a company comes through fear or competitiveness, wanting to be the best. You get a high salary as CEO because you are at risk. If you take away the risk with a golden parachute, the whole justification goes.* – Thomas J. Watson Jr., former CEO of IBM

**parachute, tin** *n.* A modest severance payment created in the face of a takeover and extended to thousands of employees. It is designed to make a hostile bidder think twice about going through with a takeover, and having to pay what amounts to thousands of unwarranted bonuses.

**paradigm shift** *n*. Term used by the CEO to tell his entire army that it is out of step, now that he hears a different drummer.

*That's the American way. If little kids don't aspire to make money like I did, what the hell good is this country?* – Lee Iacocca in 1987, defending his $20.6 million in annual compensation

*American business has got to perform differently in the 1990s. The 1980s were a time of quick bucks, greed, and a lot of corruption … There's an ethic developing that we've got to get back to basics; we've got to work and pull this country up by its bootstraps.* – Lee Iacocca, in 1990

*We used to despise anyone who drove a Cadillac because he must have been a capitalist pig who didn't care about polluting the environment. We still hate anyone who drives a Cadillac because now we all understand a Mercedes is a much classier car.* – Mark Breslin, comedy club owner

**parking lot index** *n*. Theory developed by California money manager Kenneth L. Fisher that says the easier it is to find a parking space the lousier things look for the economy. Most recessions are a year old before their effects are fully evident, but parking lots at shopping centers, hotels and airports begin to show high vacancy rates well before that – a sign that consumers are staying indoors. Also known as the couch potato index.

**parking, stock** *v*. A practice akin to parking a stolen car in a friend's driveway until the heat is off, as a means of avoiding the legal requirement that an investor declare ownership of more than 5 percent of a company's stock. Parking enables the unscrupulous raider to gain a cheap foothold in a company's stock prior to a greenmail attempt or a full-scale takeover bid.

**parvenu** *n*. A person whose wealth is of recent vintage, and who does not exhibit the good taste that would naturally come to you in a similar position.

*When a nation's elite is less than three generations removed from steerage, it cannot afford too many pretentions.* – Peter C. Newman, *Debrett's Illustrated Guide to the Canadian Establishment*

*Dig deep enough into the past of any noble family and there is … the founder with the dirty fingernails. The killer.* – Mordecai Richler, *Solomon Gursky Was Here*

**pearl-diving contest** *n*. An incentive program to whip up the sales force. In recessionary times, the reward is that you get to keep your job.

**pencil whip** *v*. An ambush by bureaucrats. Common usage: "It's a shame about Bill, he had a great proposal and he was passionate about it. But it was no use, he didn't have his facts straight. He was pencil-whipped, but good."

*Farming looks mighty easy when your plow is a pencil and you're a thousand miles from a cornfield.* – Dwight Eisenhower

**performance anxiety** *n.* Pressure to seek profit in the short term to placate the front office, which is attempting to placate stock–market analysts' demands to increase earnings per share.

*In business, we've become a country of one-night stands.* – Newton Minow, a director of Sara Lee Corp., CBS Inc. and other companies, on how performance pressure distracts CEOs from long-term priorities

**performance appraisal** *n.* An annual report card rigged to cast an overly positive or negative light on the employee, depending on whether his superior intends to promote or discharge him.

*Annual performance appraisals are the worst, most powerful force of devastation, not least because people tend to be rated on their conformity to the system instead of on trying to improve it.* – W. Edwards Deming, management theorist

**perk** *n.* Housing allowances, club memberships, corporate aircraft and other trappings of executive privilege, which function as a line of least resistance during hard times; easily shed as an act of overt contrition in order that the jobs of those who until recently benefited from them might be spared. (See **comfort zone**)

*Can't executives earning $100,000 a year afford to buy their own cars? You don't understand, respond the experts; it's not a question of affording, it's a question of feeling loved. – Fortune*

**persistence** *n*. Nine-tenths of the law.

**petroczar** *n*. An oil baron. In the Middle East, the status of a petroczar can be determined by the frequency with which he attends meetings of the Organization of Petroleum Exporting Countries. In North America, the scope of the petroczar's operations can be measured by the number of times he is called to appear before government hearings on the environment.

**philosophical difference** *n*. A point of departure reached by the executive who (a) retires gracefully before his incompetence is revealed in a full-dress firing, or (b) retires gracefully rather than exposing the incompetence of a superior during a turf war to succeed him.

**phone lag** *n*. A new affliction occasioned by the trend toward global management, whereby executives of the Dayton, Ohio, branch of the company are awakened at 3:00 a.m. by the head office in Tokyo (where the sun is shining), which has pressing news to impart. Thanks to cellular phones, faxes, voice mail and other advances in communications, the business day no longer has a beginning and end, except for those fortunate enough to employ a butler to take messages.

**phone stalling** *v*. Avoiding contact with a petitioner without giving offense, by returning his calls when you know he will be away from his station. The petitioner, clutching no fewer than three of your phone messages, appreciates that you have made the effort, and is too embarrassed by his own repeated absences to pursue the matter further. For the ploy to work you must, of course, be "in conference" when the petitioner returns *your* return calls.

**pig** *n*. An investor so intent on making the maximum profit possible that he holds off too long. While he's waiting for a stock to touch bottom, it springs to life before he can buy it cheap; or, while clinging to a stock in the hope of it reaching greater heights, it plummets.

**pine-time** *n.* The business equivalent of benching a player; an executive purgatory where managers who have been made to take the fall during **blame-time** are temporarily stripped of responsibility until they see the errors of their ways.

**pink-collar worker** *n.* A clerical worker, usually low paid, almost always female. Women's rights activists, in condemning the pay disparity between men and women in business, cite as a prime factor the concentration of women in clerical work, known as the "pink-collar ghetto."

**piss-elegant** *adj.* As with baroque art, a business proposal that is off-putting not by lack of merit, but by straining credulity through the use of extravagantly opulent artifice, grandiose nobility of phrase, and transcendent aspirations.

**planned obsolescence** *n.* Formerly a marketing practice by which business preyed on consumers. Currently a practice by which trendy consultants prey on business.

*The changes in new [car] models should be so novel and attractive as to create dissatisfaction with past models ... The laws of Paris dressmakers have come to be a factor in the automobile industry.* – Alfred P. Sloan, father of the modern General Motors Corp., in 1922

*I come from an environment where, if you see a snake, you kill it. At General Motors, if you see a snake, the first thing you do is hire a consultant on snakes.* – H. Ross Perot, a former General Motors director, in the late 1980s

**plastic** *n.* Consumer credit obtained through the use of credit cards. In the corporate sense, debt taken on with abandon and no thought to the consequences.

**plateau** *n.* A resting spot for the complacent. In careers, as well as stock prices, the plateau will be either a staging ground for a renewed assault on the mountain, or a malingering point from which the inevitable descent begins.

**plausible deniability** *n.* The act of keeping the CEO informed only of the ends, in order that he later can deny knowledge of the means.

**play, in** *adj.* The attempt by several bidders to acquire a company, in which the target firm is smashed back and forth like a squash ball to determine the superiority of one stock-jock over the others.

**plutography** *n.* The graphic depiction of wealth and power in popular journals, in the belief that *Citizen Kane* failed to cover all the bases.

**poison pill** *n.* An anti-takeover device. In its simple form, a hastily made acquisition by a firm facing a hostile takeover in order to make itself indigestible to marauders. In the more complex variation, a firm that fears for its continued independence issues warrants to stockholders giving them the right to purchase stock at a bargain price in the event a hostile party should buy a set percentage of the firm's shares – a maneuver aimed at making a takeover of the firm prohibitively expensive.

**Ponzi scheme** *n.* Named for the ingenious Boston swindler Charles Ponzi (1883-1949); any financial maneuver which requires that existing investors recover their capital with funds yet to be extracted from future investors. While Ponzi schemes are commonly thought to be of short duration, an exception may be observed in the case of deficit financing in government.

**post-30 syndrome (PTS)** *n.* A marketing label to describe consumers who are coping uneasily with the fact that they are turning into their parents: rising from bed at the hour when they used to turn in; subscribing to *National Geographic* and *National Review*; and peppering office banter with references to the antics of Saturday morning cartoon characters.

**power** *n.* Meekness in others.

*What is happiness? The feeling that power increases, that resistance is being overcome.* – Friedrich Nietzsche

*In this world, a man must either be anvil or hammer.* – Henry Wadsworth Longfellow

**power lunch** *n.* A repast where food is an afterthought to intense strategizing, dealmaking and negotiation; frequently cited as a make-it-or-break-it opportunity to favorably impress a superior.

*Don't stare at other diners' breasts.* – helpful advice from *The Toronto Star*

*Our own well-considered view on this subject – tainted, admittedly, by the fact that we frequent a lunch spot where the crepes are shaped like barnyard animals – is that if you think you can eat your way to the top, you belong back in MBA school. Obviously, though, you should know that a public tête-à-tête with your superior is not the place to, for instance, convince your boss to become an Amway distributor like you; talk with fettuccine in your mouth; belabor the point about how your guest's tie matches (a) the tablecloth (b) the plat du jour or (c) the mood you're in; or play the harmonica – no matter how good your friends say you are.* – *The Globe and Mail*

**price, Anything's for sale at the right** *phrase.* The defining ethic of business.

*If someone wants your grandmother more than you do, you'd sell, and so would I. But at the right moment, I'd probably buy her back, too.* – Allen Born, CEO of mining giant Amax Inc.

**pride** *n.* The mistaken impression that you are the principal agent of your undeniable success.

*The oldest rule of Wall Street: financial genius is before the fall.* – John Kenneth Galbraith

**prioritize** *v.* To assess the things to be done in order to determine which you cannot get to until tomorrow, later this week or the dawn of the next century.

**problem** *n.* A challenge. Problems are for wimps. A problem solved is regarded in retrospect as an "opportunity."

*If you've got a problem, share it. Then we all have a problem. If you don't, and it grows, it's your ass.* – John B. McCoy, chairman of Bank One Corp. of Columbus, Ohio, America's most profitable major bank

**productivity** *n.* Doing more with less.

**profit, negative** *n.* A loss. The more syllables required to describe the situation, the greater the quantity of red ink.

**promoter** *n.* A person with no visible means of success, who safeguards the nation's finances by continually reawakening the public's interest in Treasury bills. If he didn't exist, the government would be obliged to invent him.

**prospectus** *n.* The advertising flyer for an investment, revealing an embarrassment of hope and a poverty of means. (See **jury proof**)

**prudent–man rule** *n.* A legal requirement that pension fund managers invest the pensioners' money only as a prudent man would – recognizing that it would be an act of gross negligence to do for others what they would do unto themselves.

**public relations** *n.* The task of relating to the public the company's objectives, as one might relate to the sheep the responsibilities of the wolf.

*I am certain anything favorable you might write about me would only give the Communistic yellow press another opportunity to vilify and lie about me.* – Sir Herbert Holt, Canadian conglomateur

*My pappy told me never to bet my bladder against a brewery or get into an argument with people who buy ink by the barrel.* – Lane Kirkland, AFL-CIO leader

*Oliver North would make an excellent PR guy. If he's lying, he's lying very well, which would make him a highly excellent PR guy.* – Matt Zachowski, New York public relations specialist, quoted in *The Wall Street Journal*

**pure play** *n.* Capitalism's answer to monogamy: a company loyal to the one industry to which it is wedded, and disciplined enough to resist the temptation to experiment with others.

**quality control** *n.* A concept of rumored American origin, mass-marketed by the Swiss, and perfected in Japan.

*There is hardly anything in the world that some man can't make a little worse and sell a little cheaper.* – John Ruskin

*I believe the new trends include the requirement on the part of the customer that the vehicle will work.* – Sir Graham Day, chairman of U.K. automaker Rover Group, responding to the question "What will car buyers of the 1990s look for?"

*In its bid to be first, [Moli Energy Ltd. of Vancouver] put more emphasis on increasing the volume of its shipments instead of dealing with a flaw in its product. That flaw came home to haunt the company last August when a fire broke out in a phone that used Moli batteries, causing minor injuries to the user.* – The Globe and Mail

**quality time** *n.* 1. Precious moments devoted to others on the dubious assumption that others find your time as valuable as you do. 2. Time carved out of a busy and fulfilling home life, and set aside for the workplace. Perhaps only an hour or two each day, these rich moments are intended to "really count."

*He that hath wife and children hath given hostages to fortune; for they are impediments to great enterprises, either of virtue or mischief.*
– Francis Bacon

**questionable** *adj.* Euphemism employed by regulators and the media to alert investors to activity which, pending further inquiry, will prove the perpetrator worthy of stoning.

**radicalism, soft-core** *n.* A marketing technique that taps sixties-era concerns about peace, the environment, nuclear power and business amorality in order to sell products. The term was coined by *Forbes* in a 1989 article about Ben & Jerry's Homemake Inc., the Vermont-based maker of a popular line of "socially conscious" ice cream products. The firm, founded in 1978 by ex-hippies Ben Cohen and Jerry Greenfield, devotes 7.5 percent of its profits to high-profile charitable activities such as campaigns to cut U.S. defense spending and the rescue of tropical forests in the Amazon. (One of the firm's flavors is Rainforest Crunch.) The company also sells its ice cream at more than twice the price of ordinary brands.

*By exploiting the sympathies of the fifth column of fortyish journalists who used to be hipsters, Ben & Jerry's participates in a symbiotic relationship with the press: you supply the ink; we'll supply the wackiness ... The publicity pays off [even though there are] paradoxes in being a socially minded company whose sugar-laden, cholesterolly toxic products could keep heart surgeons and dentists busy for the next millennium. – Forbes*

*In the U.S., doing good has come to be, like patriotism, a favorite device of persons with something to sell. –* H.L. Mencken

**raider** *n.* An investor who never shirks his daunting responsibility to make the corporate world more efficient, at least until his efforts have been recognized by the targets of his indignation. Preferably this recognition should take the form of cash. (See **greenmail**)

*This is the exact opposite of [asset stripping]. It is taking companies which are being stifled under the bureaucracy of a large conglomerate and liberating them. –* Sir James Goldsmith, Anglo-French raider of Goodyear Tire & Rubber, Crown Zellerbach, Continental Group and other firms defending his raiding activities

*In the week of the French Revolution's bicentennial, we have an Anglo-French financier setting a historical precedent in offering to "liberate" a $21-billion corporation by breaking it up ... When Sir James Goldsmith, in the revolutionary tradition, talks of his plans for liberating [Britain's] BAT Industries, it is like Jean-Paul Marat talking of the splendor of Dr. Guillotin's invention. "The mecha-*

*nism falls like thunder; the head flies off; blood spurts; the man is no more."* – Peter Cook, editor, *The Globe and Mail's Report on Business*

**ratio, debt-equity** *n*. A vital sign of a company's health. As a general rule, a firm's bankers and investors become concerned when the level of debt rises to more than 50 percent of equity.

**rationalization** *n*. An exercise in drastically reducing an operation – through asset sales and layoffs – to the size at which it was last considered rational.

**reality check** *n*. A way of curbing blue-sky conceptualizing that threatens to get serious. In meetings of planners, the accounting-minded participant eventually will feel compelled to raise his hands in the time-out signal, and say that while these grandiose schemes are all fine and good, "who's going to pay for them?"

**red chip** *n*. Shares in a blue-chip Asian firm, such as Toshiba or Sony.

**Red Cross money** *n*. Bailout funding extended as a philanthropic gesture to a venerable or high-class firm that has gotten into trouble, with no expectation on the part of the donors that they will ever see their money again. Two such efforts in the 1980s include the attempt by prominent Canadian financiers to rescue publisher Jack McClelland and architect Arthur Erickson.

**redeploy** *v*. To rechannel assets from one operation to another. Also, to find a home for an accumulation of profits which must be reinvested or lost to the taxman – commonly accomplished when a company buys another company that it does not know how to run.

*A company with more cash than it needs more often than not uses it in such a way as to reverse the problem.* – Malcolm Forbes

**reference** *v*. To mention in dispatches; to highlight a topic in a document, video or other formal communication. Comon usage: "Should we reference our new Riverside plant in the annual report?" "Sorry, Bill, I meant to reference you on that."

**reformulation, product** *n*. Now with oat bran!

**registered representative** *n*. An investment world salesperson. A person so titled is registered by his firm to call you at the office and make representations as to why you should act quickly on United Consolidated Guano Mines Corp. and other investment opportunities.

**reorganization, Chapter 11** *n*. As the sky darkens with vultures, the recruitment of a bankruptcy judge to act as scarecrow.

**reposition** *n*. The second life of the hula hoop as a weight-reduction device.

**respect** *n*. Customary and sensible deference shown to authority figures who stand between you and the good life – individuals you otherwise would not entrust with the safe-keeping of your dog.

**R&D** *v.* Restrain and diminish. Even in buoyant times, care must be taken to keep research and development costs in check. Having money tied up in the laboratory curtails one's opportunities to wolf down overpriced acquisitions that happen along.

**restructuring** *n.* An attempt at self-redemption, in which everyone and everything is moved up, down or sideways, and then given a new name to see if the firm works better that way.

*We tend to meet any new situation by reorganization and attribute to this the illusion that progress is being made.* – Petronius Arbiter, A.D. 66

**rightsizing** *n.* A reconfiguration of the human resources complement by which employees are bidden to walk the plank in sufficient number to correct the imbalance between workers and profits. "Wrongsizing," it follows, is an ill-advised build-up of staff in anticipation of robust profits that fail to materialize.

**ROI** *n.* In French, a sovereign or king; in English, an acronym for return on investment. More proof of the similarity between the two languages.

**rumortrage** *n.* 1. Speculation in securities issued by companies rumored to be the imminent target of a takeover attempt. 2. An urgent report making the rounds in the Chicago Mercantile Exchange cafeteria to the effect that wheat has been found to hold a cure for baldness.

**safety-related occurrence** *n*. An accident in the work-place.

**salary** *n*. Originally a Latin term, "salt money" – the wages paid to Roman soldiers. Today, salt, which costs about a dollar per kilogram, is found in great abundance. So is the employee of the average corporation, who is valued accordingly.

**salesman** *n*. The individual we blame for self-inflicted wounds of a fiscal nature.

*His name was George F. Babbitt ... and he made nothing in particular, neither butter nor poetry, but he was nimble in the calling of selling houses for more than people could afford to pay.* – Sinclair Lewis

**Saturday night special** *n.* A takeover made quickly, so as to catch the defenders of a target company unawares.

**savings and loan** *n.* A device ideally suited to the transfer of funds (a) from depositors to ventures associated with the institution's controlling shareholder; and (b) from taxpayers to the above depositors, whose funds have become irretrievably lost in transit.

*What is robbing a bank compared with founding a bank?* – Bertolt Brecht

*It's now reached the point that if you buy a toaster you get a free Savings and Loan.* – Senator Lloyd Bentsen, chairman of the senate finance committee

**school of business** *n.* 1. Often, as in the case of elite universities, a graduate school endowed by a deceased entrepreneur, whose raw methods would have disqualified him from so much as a teaching assistantship there. 2. An academy teaching respect for the utility of quantitative analysis and theoretical management models in solving corporate problems. Not to be confused with the school of hard knocks, an academy teaching respect for getting it right the first time or you'll lose the house, the car and the start-up capital you borrowed from your mother.

**scorched-earth policy** *n.* An anti-takeover effort in which a target firm sells off the assets that have earned it the unwelcome advances of suitors, thereby reducing the firm to a pile of ashes for which its shareholders can only wish someone will make an offer.

**secretary** *n.* The person to consult when checking up on the career status of fellow executives. Best not to inquire about your own prospects.

**selective disengagement** *n.* Subsequent to the CEO's unveiling of his new vision for the company, a manager's decision to gradually dissociate from colleagues exhibiting a tendency to cling to the old vision. In extreme cases, this may require a change of squash partner.

**self-dealing** *n.* Financial onanism; the illicit use of corporate assets for the exclusive gain of the controlling shareholder.

**service, customer** *n.* Department that functions to avoid repeat sales by failing to satisfy customer requests for information and repairs.

*If we aren't customer-driven, our cars won't be, either.* – Donald E. Petersen, former CEO of Ford Motor Co.

*We don't have to care. We're the phone company.* – Lily Tomlin

*The scientific theory I like is that the rings of Saturn are composed entirely of lost airline luggage.* – Mark Russell

**service economy** *n.* An economy of shopkeepers. Also lawyers, accountants, consultants, pastry chefs, doormen, parking garage attendants and people who command $120 an hour to reorganize your closets.

*Are we going to be a services power? The double-cheeseburger-hold-the-mayo kings of the whole world?* – Lee Iacocca

*No matter what you think about the importance of health care, Americans are not going to raise their standard of living by giving each other heart transplants. Suing each other is a lot of fun, but it is not productive. In any case the rest of the world would be too smart to import our legal system. So what's left? ... Manufactur-*ing. *We're going to have to make things to survive.* – economist Lester Thurow, dean of business at the Massachusetts Institute of Technology

**sex without marriage** *n.* Prolonged merger negotiations that fail to culminate in a merger.

**shakeout** *n.* An earthquake-like disturbance in an industry overcrowded with competitors, claiming victims among all firms save those with the soundest foundations.

**shallow** *adj.* Term for a vessel that can hold only one person's ideas, none of them yours.

**shark repellent** *n.* A pungent aroma released by the target of a hostile takeover, which, if effective, will encourage the predator to seek its meal elsewhere. Types of repellent abound, and are by no means limited to the **poison pill** and the target's indiscretion in circulating reports about the raider's track record some years earlier as the operator of a brothel two blocks from St. Peter's Square.

**shopping, recreational** *n.* Shopping not for necessity or to satisfy a hedonistic urge to accumulate, but merely because it is there, and is a more reliable, pleasurable experience than anything aside from sleep. America's leading home remedy for depression.

*There is no doubt about it, there is no pleasure like it, the sudden splendid spending of money and we spent it.* – Gertrude Stein

**shotgun wedding** *n.* The reluctant marriage of a manufacturer who has gotten a supplier into trouble by convincing it to go all the way in undertaking a costly expansion to supply the manufacturer's new product line.

**shrinkage** *n.* Disappearance of inventory to customer or employee basements.

*The other day our towels told us that some of them were being kidnapped and taken to faraway places. So we adopted some new ones and now everyone is happy again. Now you wouldn't want to break up a new family, would you? Thank you for caring.* – notice posted in every room at the Holiday Inn World's Fair hotel in Knoxville, Tennessee

**significant negative adjustment** *n.* An abrupt revision of previous financial statements to jibe with the reality of that period. Common usage: "In light of a careful reexamination of our records, the company's financial position in the third quarter of last year must be restated as follows: The profit we reported was a loss; the warehouses we thought were full were empty; the receivables we expected to collect turn out to be due in 2007; and the chief accountant in our employ at that time now resides in Tierra del Fuego."

**sincerity** *n.* The belief that Alan Alda would last for more than ten minutes as president of General Motors.

**single–issue warrior** *n.* An executive who is obsessed with but one pet goal, to the exclusion of other issues such as running the company.

**sixtysomething** *n.* A subversive mental condition, the chief symptom of which is a premature longing for retirement.

**skin** *n*. Officewear.

*To advance rapidly, you need to create an image that will distinguish you from your colleagues, a positive can-do image that will force people around you — and several ranks above you — to know who you are … At IBM Corp., where the dress code was conservative, it would have been silly to wear patterned shirts and loud sports coats. I wore the dark suits, but they were European tailored; I wore white shirts, but mine had French cuffs.* — Paul Stern, CEO of Northern Telecom Ltd., on the management skills that play a key role in being promoted, in his book, *Straight to the Top*

**sleeping beauty** *n*. A company ripe for takeover, thus marked because it has a lot of underperforming assets, its shares are bargain-priced, and its management has not erected takeover defenses.

**smoking gun** *n*. The key piece of documentary evidence, thought to have been destroyed but preserved in a middle manager's ass-covering file, which secures the conviction of a person or company guilty of a corporate crime.

*My boy, never write a letter if you can help it, and never destroy one.* — Sir John A. Macdonald, first prime minister of Canada, whose government fell soon after his telegram to a railway baron pleading for more campaign funds ("I must have another $10,000") was revealed in the press

**snooze** *n.* Any unarresting memo, report or proposal. In particular, a sales presentation that fails to shake anyone from the impression that the perpetrator could not sell a Japanese car in Yokohama – or even New York – if his life depended on it.

**social distancing** *n.* The practice of avoiding contact with a fellow executive tainted with failure and about to be mushroomed, lest you suffer a similar fate by association.

**social registry factor** *n.* An indicator of the resistance level of a takeover target. Target companies with wealthy, well-connected management are more likely to engage in friendly takeover talks, while firms whose directors have modest backgrounds are more likely to fight a takeover vigorously. Directors with career options outside the company are less likely to resist.

**socialism, Ramada** *n.* Socialist policies that have been diluted in recognition of capitalism's new credibility with voters in most Western industrial nations. The term was coined in the U.K. and is also applicable to the new "market-oriented" ever-less-Left leanings of the U.S. Democratic Party and Canada's New Democratic Party.

**soft target** *n.* In a downsizing exercise, bloated company divisions or employee groups that can be shrunk with a minimum of disruption.

**sovereign risk** *n.* A loan for which a developing nation was put up as collateral.

*Somehow the conventional wisdom of 200 million sullen South Americans sweating away in the hot sun for the next decade to earn the interest on their debt so Citicorp can raise its dividend twice a year does not square with my image of political reality.* – Barton Biggs, a managing director of investment banking firm Morgan Stanley

**spearhead** *v.* The person who lives to enjoy the reputation of having spearheaded a successful project almost certainly shouted his orders from the rear, thereby avoiding being counted among the front-line casualties that every daring venture claims.

**speculation** *n.* A reckless, irresponsible and avaricious gamble that does not pay off, as opposed to an "investment," which does.

*Speculation is the romance of trade, and casts contempt upon all its sober realities. It renders the stock-jobber a magician, and the Exchange a land of enchantment.* – Washington Irving

*The blind do not, in fact, lead the blind, but the gullible do gull the gullible. It is the confidence that speculators have in their own bad judgment that inspires confidence in others. So the speculators join those whom they have inspired in hope and avarice and are there with them holding the bag at the end. Then they are revealed for what they always were, which is not much.* – John Kenneth Galbraith, reflecting on the Hunt brothers' early-1980s debacle in attempting to corner the market in silver

**speed money** *n.* A bribe paid to expedite the transport of goods, recognizing that in some countries bribery is a way of life at the border stations as well as the legislature.

**speed racing** *n.* An affliction of the executive cocaine addict.

*The ones who had [cocaine] all the time were the old guys, the 40- and 50-year-olds, out in the front office, the bosses and traders who would come in looking devastated and suddenly, after a trip to the men's room, would jabber, grab phones and rush from desk to desk.* – Jimmy Breslin

**stick-to-your-knitting strategy** *n.* A policy of refusing to diversify; sticking to the one thing you're good at. Possibly the most successful strategy in the history of business, honored more in the breach than the observance. Even companies that subscribe to it find eventually that they must redeploy the profits it brings, and end up diversifying into new and treacherous realms despite everything that previous experience has taught them. (See **pure play**)

*Put all your eggs in one basket – [and] watch that basket! –* Mark Twain

*When a management with a reputation for brilliance tackles a business with a reputation for bad economics, it is the reputation of the business that remains intact. I just wish I hadn't been so energetic in creating examples. My behavior has matched that admitted by Mae West: "I was Snow White, but I drifted." –* Warren Buffett

**stock market** *n.* A den of equities, where the person who manages to look smart for more than ten minutes probably deserves his reputation for sagacity.

*If you don't know who you are, the stock market is an expensive place to find out. –* "Adam Smith" (Jerry Goodman)

**strategic planning** *n.* Planning undertaken with care and deliberation, as opposed to normal planning.

*Hasty and adventurous schemes are at first view very flattering, in execution difficult, and in the issue disastrous. –* Titus Livy

*If we ever have a plan, we're screwed. –* Paul Newman, salad-oil entrepreneur

**strategic profile** *n*. An elaborately conceived design of what the firm ideally should look like, hurriedly constructed to explain the recently rushed sale of large portions of the company. The portions were sold not because they were lame, or as a means of raising desperately needed cash, but because they no longer fit the strategic profile.

**streamline** *v*. Slash and burn, in the form of layoffs, sale of assets, closure of plants and other draconian measures, and usually announced in an upbeat way.

*As we prepare for further technological advancements in the 1990s [so far, so good], we anticipate that we will require fewer manufacturing people [whew, glad I'm in sales] and also require different manufacturing, selling [oh God] and equipment servicing skills [oh God, that's everybody] ... to assure continued strong revenue and earnings growth.* – postage meter maker Pitney Bowes Inc., announcing in 1989 a cut of 1,500 jobs

**street name** *n*. An investment registered in the name of your broker, thereby entrusting it to his haphazard custody rather than yours.

**stress management** *n*. A program of on-site nutrition counseling, fitness breaks and other measures designed to reduce tension levels in the workplace. At less progressive companies, it falls to the employee to manage his own stress level. This can be accomplished by enrollment into stress clinics, the use of special breathing exercises and the adoption of proper eating and sleeping habits, or by attaching a small plastic explosive device to your boss's car.

*If you look like your passport photo, you need the trip.* – Gordon Goss and Valerie Thornton, editors, *Overheard at the Square Dance*


**subsidy** *n.* A government grant, interest-free loan, tax break or suspension of regulations unfairly extended to a competitor. (See **level playing field**)

*The business of government is to keep the government out of business — that is, unless business needs government aid.* – Will Rogers


**success** *n.* The rare confluence of a good idea, superb execution and kind fate, producing the unhappy result of still grander but less sound designs being attempted. (See **failure**)

*Success is overrated. Everyone craves it despite daily proof that man's real genius lies in quite the opposite direction. Incompetence is what we are good at: it is the quality that marks us off from animals and we should learn to revere it.* – Stephen Pile, *The Incomplete Book of Failures: The Official Handbook of the Not-Terribly-Good Club*

**succession** *n.* The coronation of a new absolute ruler, whose shortcomings soon will no longer be the subject of mere speculation.

*The question "Who ought to be boss?" is like asking "Who ought to be tenor in the quartet?" Obviously, the man who can sing tenor.* – Henry Ford

*Now that I was on top, I knew others would want to topple me ... I believe in practising the S.O.B.'s Golden Rule: Expect others to do unto you what you would do to them.* – Allen Neuharth, former CEO of Gannett Co., *Confessions of an S.O.B.*

**suicide pill** *n.* An acquisition made in order to render a potential takeover target unattractive to suitors, the debt from which proves unwieldy.

**suit** *n.* Hard-nosed executive, usually dispatched from the front office, as opposed to casually dressed creative types who do the real damage. People who don't appreciate him see the suit's job as whipping a little discipline, conformity and despair on people who are trying to get their work done. (See **anti-suit**)

**suit, empty** *n.* A close cousin of the traditional yes-man, except that this individual, while pandering to the brass, also strives mightily to create the appearance of possessing leadership qualities. This trait manifests itself in the fine tailoring of the individual's wardrobe, a slavish devotion to conducting business according to the rules of the corporate culture and a well-developed skill in robbing subordinates of credit for ideas that catch on with top management. When the empty suit moves on – and usually up – no one can remember what he or she did all day.

*The empty suit has ample opportunity to focus on doing the correct thing, not as a means of getting real work done, but as an end in itself. If the standard corporate drill is to have a weekly meeting with staff, he will have that meeting faithfully every Wednesday, whether or not anything is accomplished. Usually nothing is, in part because the suit doesn't want to say yea or nay. – Fortune*

**summit** *n.* An annual gathering of executives at a liberating remove from head office, where participants are implored to reveal the enormity of their discontent and their brave new ideas for the future – save any that conflict with the master vision for the company unveiled on this same occasion by the CEO.

*When I want your opinion, I'll give it to you.* – Samuel Goldwyn

**supply and demand, law of** *n.* The unerring instinct of consumers to purchase ever increasing quantities of an item until it becomes too expensive to buy.

*People will buy anything that's one to a customer.* – Sinclair Lewis

**synergy** *n.* The advertised benefits of merging disparate entities (companies or individuals) into an idle whole, calling forth the image of painted profits upon a painted ocean.

**tailgating factor** *n.* Theory advanced by Jerrold Richards of Hood River, Oregon, which holds that as recession looms, drivers' increasing preoccupation with staving off career or personal-finance disaster accounts for the reduction in space between cars on the freeway.

**takeover, creeping** *n.* A takeover accomplished by acquiring small amounts of stock in the target firm over a long period of time; the corporate finance version of being nibbled to death by ducks.

**takeover, hostile** *n*. The unreasonable attempt by a company to prevent a marauder from demonstrating how well run the firm had been prior to its appearance.

*Hostile corporate takeovers … may be the most glaring example of organizing the firing squad into a circle … Hostile takeovers, as ends in themselves, typically combine zero productive enhancement with the redeeming social value of a feeding frenzy.* – Norman Augustine, CEO of aerospace giant Martin Marietta Corp., the victim of a failed hostile takeover attempt in the early 1980s

**takeover, reverse** *n*. The elephant swallowed by the ant.

**tax avoidance** *n*. Our ship registered in Panama, operated by a subsidiary incorporated in Venezuela.

**tax evasion** *n*. Undeclared receipts and over-declared invoices.

**tax-loss carryforward** *n*. Last year's red ink applied against this year's black ink.

**tax shelter** *n*. A film starring Donald Sutherland and Harvey Korman, shot on location in mainland China with a French crew, and financed by dentists.

**team player** *n.* 1. A manager who does not let the urgings of his ego intrude on the smooth functioning of the group. 2. A manager who does not let the urgings of his conscience intrude on the unsavory practices of the group.

*To get along, go along.* – dictum of Sam Rayburn when he was Speaker of the House of Representatives

**tech angst** *n.* Fear of automation among consumers, as exhibited by their initial reluctance to put their trust in automated teller machines. Citibank's halfhearted response to the problem was to unveil a network of ATMs in New York City that speak English, Cantonese and Spanish, but are not equipped to handle "F'r chrissakes, fugedebadit," and other quaint idioms of the Bronx dialect.

**tennis–court justice** *n.* Light sentences meted out to white-collar criminals, and served in a Club Med-like setting. To paraphrase Stalin, a grocery store holdup in Queen's is a tragedy; 41 million liters of oil off the coast of Alaska is a statistic.

**tight money policy** *n.* A brake to inflationary pressures in the economy, which a nation's central bank applies by raising the rate of interest on funds it lends to banks, and by cutting the power supply to the plants where currency is printed.

**tire-kicker** *n*. A prospective buyer who is not prepared to lay down his cash just yet – even after asking you to bring down all the heavy objects from the high shelves. A prospective acquisitor who asks for detailed information about a company on the auction block, but only out of idle curiosity or a bid to obtain sensitive information about a competitor.

**top-down** *adj*. The traditional reporting system, in which decisions made at the top are passed down through the ranks, becoming less clear and more poorly enforced as they journey to the plant floor.

**top line** *n*. Total sales or revenue. It will be observed that gratifying growth in this figure does not always translate into growth in the bottom line. The derisive term "top-line manager" applies to the manager intent on swelling the size of the business without regard to the attendant rise in expenses – and the negative impact this has on the bottom line.

**tort-ure** *v*. To litigate with extreme prejudice.

**tough but fair** *phrase*. Term applied to an executive whose reputation for ruthlessness is somewhat skewed by arbitrary acts of kindness toward pets and small children.

*Every successful enterprise requires three men – a dreamer, a businessman, and a son-of-a-bitch.* – Peter McArthur, turn-of-the-century British newspaper publisher

*The meek shall inherit the earth, but not the mineral rights.* —
J. Paul Getty

**transition period, We face a challenging** *phrase*. Translation: As we embark on this next corporate expedition,
employees may want to notify their next of kin.

**tree hugger** *n*. 1. A zealous **green.** 2. A loyal company man
whose reward for putting in twenty or thirty years at the
same firm is to be shunned by recruiters because he lacks
varied career experience.

*A tree hugger is increasingly seen as ... Narrow in experience and
someone who's fearful of the unknown.* – Jacques Lapointe, president of Retail Recruiters International Inc.

**trickle-down theory** *n*. An economic doctrine: Only as the
comfortable are permitted to become more comfortable will
they sweep larger table scraps into the waiting mouths
below.

*I've learned that the trickle-down theory is warm, wet and amber-
colored.* – unemployed worker in Edmonton, Alberta,
responding to a federal budget that granted investors the
right to enjoy their first $500,000 worth of capital gains on
investments free of tax

**Trojan horse** *n.* An illicit computer program (also known as a virus) planted in a legitimate one by a white-collar criminal in order to sabotage a computer system, or to command illegal transfers of corporate funds and other assets.

**Trojan horse issue** *n.* In Canada, a newly created class of shares, usually nonvoting, which enable foreign investors to acquire equity in a Canadian firm without breaching laws forbidding offshore ownership.

**trophy wife** *n.* The CEO's stunning second wife, twenty years younger than her predecessor, who has exchanged a modeling career for that of teaching her new charge how to dress, where to eat, which proper charities to favor and the fine points of holding a backyard party for 300. (See **Jennifer syndrome**)

**Trump complex** *n.* A simple character trait of the investor who finds that an acquisition lacks meaning until it has been rechristened in his likeness.

*Hoy-day, what a sweep of vanity comes this way!* – William Shakespeare

**turd in the plaza** *n.* The piece of ugly, intimidating, incomprehensible sculpture in front of the company's new headquarters.

**turkey** *n.* 1. An investment whose efforts at flight are as painful to observe as the dog's attempts at song. 2. A person in possession of such an investment.

**turnover** *n.* The rate at which employees part with companies.

**turtle mode** *n.* A cutback regime implemented in response to recessionary storm warnings.

**ubiquity factor** *n.* The tendency for people who are always hanging around to get ahead, even if it is not clear what they are contributing; the equal but opposite tendency for your interests to be jeopardized by a decision reached at the only meeting you weren't able to attend.

*Showing up is 80 percent of life.* – Woody Allen

**underground economy** *n.* The cottage you built for your neighbor, the motor home he then donated to his cousin, the leather jackets with which that man then outfitted your family.

**underperforming asset** *n.* An asset that has not exceeded management's limitations.

*If you can't fix it, sell it. If you can't sell it, shoot it.* – Allen Born, CEO of Amax Inc.

**unusual** *adj.* A non-libelous media term signaling a craven breach of accounting standards in a corporate financial statement. Synonyms include "irregular" and "confusing."

**upscale** *adj.* Denoting a person of high income and refined taste, or an item targeted at such a person. The targets are not always people. In 1985, Ralston-Purina Co. introduced a luxury pet food called Catviar.

*Too many people. We must be doing something wrong.* – Harold Ross, on learning that the circulation of *The New Yorker* had risen above 300,000.

**upside potential** *n.* Then again, you could become obscenely rich. (See **downside risk**)

**vaporware** *n.* A promised advance in new technology that fails to materialize. Common among computer and other high-tech firms that attract orders for heralded breakthroughs that never emerge from the lab.

**velvet coffin** *n.* A corporate practice of maintaining lifetime employment; usually associated with paternalistic, family-owned businesses. This is the first thing to be buried in the event of a takeover.

**vendor financing** *n.* The house you sold, upon which you hold the mortgage.

**vice-president** *n.* The first rung on the ladder out of middle-management serfdom. Also, often the last, since the wise CEO knows it is useful to occasionally fire a vice-president in order to encourage the rest.

*There is nothing wrong with the average corporation that could not be solved by firing a passel of vice-presidents.* – Peter Drucker

**vision** *n.* An idea in black tie. No self-respecting businessperson gets by on hunches anymore; even George Bush now relies on "the vision thing."

**visionary** *n.* A leader whom it pleases the shareholders to support. To be a visionary in more than his own mind, a leader must maintain a track record of success. Napoleon was a visionary for a while, then he wasn't, then he was again, then he died on a remote island. His vision didn't change a whole lot, only the results.

**visioning** *v.* The process of conceiving the future. For the gas station owner, this means eyeballing the new station on the opposite corner, and deciding to install flower beds and a car wash. At the higher reaches, visioning takes the form of a brainstorming session at a luxurious retreat, where executives give speeches in the hope of future considerations. At poolside, the vision that evolves is: "Bill's presentation showed a lot of moxie, but it still won't get him the Frankfurt posting."

**vitamin pill** *n.* An anti-takeover device by which a firm hoping to thwart a suitor makes an acquisition designed to quickly enrich earnings and drive up its stock price.

**voice** *n.* An act of ventriloquism in which a product makes itself known in quarters where it has not yet appeared – either by advertising or word of mouth.

*Business today consists in persuading crowds.* – Gerald Stanley Lee

**vulture fund** *n.* A mutual fund that invests in bargain-priced securities issued by ailing companies.

**wallet biopsy** *n.* A preoperative procedure performed in private hospitals to determine the likely duration of a patient's stay.

**wallflower** *n.* A stock of sensible bearing but plain appearance, ignored for now, yet hopeful of someday meeting an investor with similar qualities.

**white knight** *n.* The least-hated suitor.

**window of opportunity** *n.* An aperture that opens onto an idyllic scene of a rainbow terminating in a pot of gold, through which one is obliged to jump before the shutter closes and everything goes black again.

**work** *n.* An activity designed to make life pleasurable and fulfilling, as hunting for food was in earlier times.

*If hard work were such a wonderful thing, surely the rich would have kept it all to themselves.* – Lane Kirkland, labor leader

**work ethic** *n.* The belief that if other people tried it, they would find hard work to be as spiritually ennobling as you do.

*Americans work to make money and to win respect, but to some extent our culture says that you work hard so eventually you won't have to work. You struggle for a degree so that you can get out of the factory, you scrimp and save so that you can retire early. I'm sure the Japanese don't love to sweat any more than the rest of us, but the basic calculation seems different [there]. They work because that is their duty to a tight-knit, homogeneous society. They work ... to keep on working.* – James Fallows, *Atlantic Monthly*

**work surface** *n.* An immoderately priced desk.

**write-off** *n.* The act of putting an underperforming asset out of the company's misery by formally erasing its value in the financial statements.

*It is generally considered more comfortable to take a dog's tail off all at once rather than an inch at a time.* – Charles Brown, chairman of AT&T Corp., explaining the rationale for his firm's $5.2-billion write-off in 1983

**wrong, I'm not sure what went** *phrase.* Translation: What you don't know won't hurt me.

**yes-man** *n.* A species of invertebrate whose presence is indispensable to the smooth functioning of an organization.

*Woe unto you, when all men shall speak well of you.* – Luke 6:26

*I don't want any yes-men in this organization. I want people to speak their minds – even if it does cost them their jobs.* – Samuel Goldwyn

**yield** *n.* The return surrendered by an investment in compensation for the sleep it has cost you.

**young indicted professional (yippie)** *n.* Demographic term for Wall Street traders and lawyers barely out of adolescence who have been swept up by their suspenders in the insider-trading dragnet.

**young upwardly mobile Marxist (yummie)** *n.* Newly materialistic citizen emerging in the USSR and Eastern Europe, imitating Western consumeristic cravings for designer duds and electronic hardware.

**young urban pestilence (yuppie)** *n.* A revel without a cause.

*Of course, yuppies are against nuclear war. It interferes with their career plans.* – Abbie Hoffman

**zircon in the rough** *n*. A colleague who at first glance appears to be possessed of exceedingly modest talents, a perception confirmed on closer inspection.

# Index to Quoted Subjects